FOR
PREACHERS
ONLY

FOR PREACHERS ONLY

Endorsed by the United Pentecostal Church as required reading for ministers, this book delivers important, real-life insights for today's minister.

The Preacher's Call

The Minister As a Person

The Preacher and His Home

Getting Started in the Ministry

The Minister and His Preaching

The Minister and Divine Leadership

The Minister and Authority

J. T. PUGH

For Preachers Only

by J. T. Pugh

©1971 Word Aflame® Press
  Hazelwood, MO 63042-2299

Reprint History: 1975, 1979, 1981, 1983, 1986, 1988, 1990, 1993,
            1996, 1999
Second edition © 2001 Word Aflame® Press, 2004, 2007, 2010

Cover Design: Paul Povolni

Printed in United States of America

WORD AFLAME PRESS
8855 Dunn Road, Hazelwood, MO 63042
www.pentecostalpublishing.com

Library of Congress Cataloging-in-Publication Data

Pugh, J. T., 1923–2010
    For preachers only.

    Reprint. Originally published: Hazelwood, MO. :
Pentecostal Pub. House, 1971.
    1. Pastoral theology. 2. Clergy—Office. I. Title.
BV4011.P84   1986   253   86-10976
ISBN 0-912315-35-0

Contents

Introduction

At age seventeen I heard the character of a minister vindicated by the statement, "He is a gracious Southern gentleman." Though I was young in years, these words left me with a feeling that the compliment just heard was worth striving for. It goes without saying that every minister is expected to be a Christian gentleman. The definition of a gentleman is "a man of good birth and social standing; a well-bred and courteous man." The Scriptures concede, "David behaved himself wisely," and finally in the last verse of the chapter the author recorded, "David behaved himself more wisely." (See I Samuel 18:14, 30.) If wisdom and gentleness played their part in elevating David to the throne of Israel, we conclude that their exhibition in the life and relations of a Pentecostal minister will certainly be most helpful.

The preacher who "loses his life" in the interest of others will find it flowing back to him in warm and willing response. We refer to an unselfish interest in others' welfare because it is the heart of courteous and proper conduct. It should not be hard to carry out Peter's command to be courteous (I Peter 3:8) when there is nothing but goodwill in our hearts for all people. For this reason, many older and seasoned ministers in Pentecost, though some have been untrained in the finer points of etiquette, have been able to move among people with poise and sure grace that was worthy of the dignity of their office.

However, since to my knowledge a code of ministerial ethics for Pentecostals has not as yet been drawn up and published in book form, I now attempt to do so. I make such an attempt because other books that deal with this subject, while helpful and instructive, do not comprehend the needs of the Pentecostal minister. The younger minister and the ministerial student can proceed with more assurance if a norm of conduct is available in book form. Observations of others, while undeniably good, take longer to receive. Hence, in the absence of a written work, the accumulation of needed knowledge might be spread out over many years.

The information on the following pages is the result of much observation on my part for twenty-three years. Opinions of my fellow ministers, gathered in many conversations and ministerial gatherings, I pass on to you. If these studies are a help and blessing to anyone, the appreciative gesture must go to many of the ministers who make up the fellowship of the United Pentecostal Church International. Since the source of material is so broad and general, it is impossible to cite any definite authority. Moreover, I certainly want to make clear that I do not consider this material a rebuke; it is simply the opinion of ministers such as the reader.

So I pass on to you a collection garnered from ministers across twenty-three years of blessed fellowship. I offer it with the prayerful hope that it might be a blessing.

1

The Preacher's Call

The most solemnly important duties that anyone can undertake are involved in the office and work of a minister of the gospel. This point is clear when we recognize the titles by which the Bible designates a minister. He is a "watchman," a "witness," a "teacher," a "pastor," an "evangelist," a "minister of Christ," an "ambassador for Christ," and many other appellations equally significant. Who can doubt the weighty responsibility conferred by the preaching of the gospel?

Into this office no one may enter unbidden. "And no man taketh this honour unto himself, but he that is called of God, as was Aaron" (Hebrews 5:4). The United Pentecostal Church recognizes the necessity of a divine call, and in her economy it is considered improper and dishonest for anyone to take upon himself the office of public preaching or divine administration before he is divinely called. Licensing and ordination are administered upon the assumption that the selecting hand of God has preceded the hands of the presbytery. No accrediting commission that the church might convey is valid in God's sight unless the applicant for the ministry knows and feels in his own heart that he has been called by God to preach.

Thus preaching is not altogether a learned profession. We can refer to it as a profession in that it should carry with it ethics and respect peculiar to its field. But the holy ministry is more than a profession. It is a vocation and more, a sacred call. It is not a pursuit chosen from among many equally obligatory, but one accepted upon the persuasion and conviction that "I have been called to preach." While Christ was upon this earth, He selected from a larger group of disciples those who were later to minister the Word, but He did not transfer to them the right of appointing their successors. This prerogative He still retains, and He calls His ministers now, as He did then.

There Must Be a Definite Call

The problems and discouragements associated with the ministry make it imperative that every Pentecostal preacher be convinced of his calling. More than one good person has given up under fire and returned to secular work in grave doubt that he was ever called to preach. To exert pressure upon a likely ministerial prospect to announce his call immediately is an unjust and dangerous practice. This decision is one that the prospect must arrive at for himself. Thus he approaches the sacred grounds of divine choice and human will. In this place there is only room for one person and his God. The recognition that this decision will involve the rest of his life should caution all not to meddle with a matter so far-reaching and personal. Perhaps there are some who struggle along with a haunting doubt that they were ever called of God. If they resign from the ministry, they face an awkward situation under another person's ministry. It hurts a person to fail and admit that he was wrong in his aspirations. Some carry such scars to their grave. How it pays to be careful in influencing anyone to announce his call to preach!

After a person has arrived at such a decision for himself, of course, it is in order to offer all encouragement to qualify himself and pursue his calling heartily. Most of the time a person who has a real call from God becomes willing and eager to do just that. Necessity is laid upon him. His choice is not a preference among alternatives. Ultimately he has no alternative. The call of the eternal is in his soul. He feels very deeply that "woe is unto me, if I preach not the gospel" (I Corinthians 9:16).

Paul stated the strong impetus of his call in Colossians 1:28-29: "Whom we preach, warning every man, and teaching every man in all wisdom; that we may present every man perfect in Christ Jesus: whereunto I also labour, striving according to his working, which worketh in me mightily." We also read in II Corinthians 5:20: "Now then we are ambassadors for Christ, as though God did beseech you by us: we pray you in Christ's stead, be ye reconciled to God."

There may be diversity of opinions regarding the evidence of this call to preach. However, all can agree that there are some basic motivations inherent in truly called ministerial aspirants. One of the first evidences of a ministerial call is a strong heart hunger for a close fellowship with God.

The great majority of United Pentecostal ministers can doubtless look back to a time prior to their ministry when great burdens of prayer swept them to their knees. For most ministers those great hours and climactic days were filled with a strange loneliness, a soul hunger that only prayer and God could satisfy. In the minds of many ministers is the memory of a place where they retired in those heart-searching rendezvous with God. For some it was the church. For others it was the woods or perhaps a room at home. Certain hours are dear to many because it was the hour of their divine love feast. It was in those times and places that Jesus courted their love, as He persistently did Peter's on the windswept beach in words he was never to forget, "Peter, . . . lovest thou me?" (John 21:15-17).

One thing that accompanies the ministerial call is a new perception or evaluation of the world in general. "The things of earth grow strangely dim." The searching person will enter a new and greater wideness of spiritual comprehension. The soul moves further out, hungrily, into the stream of God's will. The once-coveted material goals of life pale in the light of eternal verities. Feeling so keenly about spiritual things now, the aspirant wonders how those about him could remain so unmoved to fervent prayer and holy endeavor. A strong awareness of Christ's coming calls for a reappraisal of all worldly associations. Earthly ambitions are viewed as folly, and carnal attainments as vanity. Measured by the weight of the judgment and the length of eternity, things once held dear lose their significance. Frequently the zest with which the secular life was pursued wanes, and the most important part of the day is that which is filled with spiritual activity. Daily, a new perception of life's extreme brevity warns him that "only what's done for Christ will last."

Certainly there are many wonderful laypersons today who have been powerfully seized by this divine craving who were never called to preach. There is no contention that such holy compulsions come only to those apprehended for the ministry, but who doubts that he who properly wears the prophet's mantle comes to a place in life where his eyes are opened to holy things as never before?

A Prevailing Passion for Lost Souls

It would be inconceivable that a person could be divinely led into the ministry without being endued with a prevailing passion for souls. Primarily, it was for the sake of others that Jesus Christ called His first disciples. (See John 4:35.) To the seventy that He sent out to preach, He said, "The harvest truly is great, but the labourers are few" (Luke 10:2). The person whom God is dealing with concerning the ministry will more than likely also be transfixed with the appalling lostness of the world. His communication will not only be perpendicular, but horizontal as well. His call from God is distinctly in relation to others. It is hard to visualize a person being called to preach who never witnesses to the lost, who does not work with seekers at the altar, or who does not weep for sinners in secret. The preacher is to preach the gospel, and the gospel is for sinners.

People of many fields feel the aptitude for their vocation in the tender years of youth. The carpenter, doctor, or mechanic feels an inclination toward his final labor perhaps years before he is employed. While preaching is not simply a vocation or a profession, who would question that some of its mighty drive stimulates the soul of God's chosen long before he acknowledges his call? Many people holding credentials with the United Pentecostal Church International today were at one time the strongest altar workers in their local church where they worshiped as laypersons. Some entered the ministry through witnessing at street meetings, or in devotional services conducted during the noon hour on their job.

Judaism was chiefly limited to a single nation. Christianity extends its sympathies and provisions alike to each individual and to all nations. It makes religion a personal business and the salvation of souls a grand object of its ministers.

Promotion of the Work of God in General

The call of God manifests itself in a fervent interest to promote the work of God in general. Janitorial work, mowing grass, and general repair work about the church have been the glad and willing choice of many before they anticipated the ministry. This is not only proper but good. Experience teaches that the best leaders come up through the ranks. Some preachers have entered their calling by way of the Sunday school class. Others have been conscientious Sunday school superintendents, and still others have been youth leaders. It is noteworthy that most of the great people of the Bible were busy when divine necessity laid hold of them. The best and most progressive preachers, it seems, have formerly been their pastor's right-hand man. They have not shirked their full responsibility in promoting the growth of their home church. Industry, ardor, and zeal have been the hallmark of God's greatest masters of the pulpit. This predisposition often makes itself apparent in the faithfulness with which the conscientious one discharges the smaller responsibilities left to his care while he is yet a layperson.

The aspiring layperson who has the fire smoldering in his bones is interested in every facet of God's work. He has a longing for the growth of his local Sunday school, a yearning for the lost about him, a concern for the mission field, and an expectant eagerness for the success of every local revival. In these inclinations, and more, he begins to show his propensity for the ministry.

As we have already discussed, acknowledging the call to preach should be left entirely to God and the candidate. Discretion would perhaps even lead the pastor to discourage the coveting layperson if his background, disposition, and circumstances stand overwhelmingly against the feasibility of such a choice. The wise pastor might justify his actions in that he has saved at least one person, and perhaps many others, from grievous spiritual hurt. If such a one really has the fire in his soul and the "go" in his heart, he will be back, and the little wait he was encouraged to take will not hinder him in the least. It is the quality more than the quantity of ministers that is needed. Ten righteous people would have saved Sodom. Jeremiah sought for one person to stand in the gap and make up the hedge to save Israel. God only needed one person like Paul to spread the gospel to parts of the world where even the screaming eagles of the Roman Empire had not been heard.

God is sovereign and appoints His own representatives, irrespective of human arrangements. However, when one is really called, those who are in sympathy with the work of the Spirit will discover it. God could instantly reveal it, as He did the call of Saul of Tarsus to Ananias, but He seldom does. It pays to beware of those who lay hands suddenly upon people. God is supernatural, but He is not foolish. A person's gift will make way for him. Some of the best preachers began their work for God and grew up into fruitfulness some time before announcing their call to preach. Matthew Simpson, a Methodist bishop in 1880, stated, "Better to dig coal in the mines or break stones on the road than to stand in the pulpit uncalled of God." In time, public proclamation will substantiate a person's call. The fire shut up in his bones will be detected by others, and soon those about him will know he is among the prophets. His life has approximated to the ministry as steel is drawn to the magnet. His desire has harmonized with the claims of the gospel.

The call may be only a vague impression at first, a kind of waking dream. This may be treated as a temptation and banished as such. This was the case with many of the best people who now stand in the holy place. While some had known for many years that they were to preach, others had no idea of such. Then gradually their minds mysteriously lingered on the subject, perhaps while they were in the midst of anxious activities for Christ's kingdom. Some have started up from a pleasant reverie and found themselves addressing an imaginary congregation. In spite of unbelief, the subject insistently impressed them until it created the conviction that God might be calling them to His work. Finally, they knew He had called them and at length came the feeling, "Woe is me if I preach not the gospel."

Getting Started

A clear understanding of divine things, a ready utterance, tact, and especially success in doing good go a long way toward a good start in the ministry. "Fruits" are particularly convincing. But not everyone is blessed with a glib tongue from the start. It was said of Dwight Moody that his friends advised him not to speak in public lest he offend some of the brethren. So he went into the streets and lanes, talked to the children, and invited them into an old, forsaken room that he lighted with a tallow candle. But his efforts were blessed, and he became more than an acknowledged preacher. While at the start, some of the outward circumstances conducive to a successful ministry might be lacking, the inward witness of those who are truly called is correspondingly as strong. In time people will have to say, "It is the LORD: let him do what seemeth good." (See I Samuel 3:18.) God's ways are not always our ways.

The ministry occupies a large field and requires a variety of abilities. Thus some circumstances yield themselves more readily to plain, dedicated, common-sense men than to the more bookish and profound. Education has been known to disqualify some for the highest usefulness in certain places because it created a mutual aversion between the minister and his congregation. They just did not talk the same language. There is always a place for everyone who is truly called of God to preach, or God would not have called him.

A great supply of conflicting advice is given to candidates; some urge them to leave all and preach at once, while others suggest a waiting period. Bible college is always a possibility and quite often the desire of a prospective preacher. He must think and pray himself out of any quandary, perhaps being guided by the advice of one or two concerned ministers whose judgment is reliable. Of course, this still does not eliminate all the questions. Should the aspirant quit his job and launch immediately into the work? Should he keep his job and preach occasionally or as often as the opportunity presents itself? Should he make plans to attend Bible college immediately? He had better count the cost and weigh these things before he announces his call. It is much better to be a good teacher, a strong and helpful exhorter, following his own convictions and adaptations, than become an inefficient preacher by following the opinions of many. He knows his own convictions, affinities and circumstances, and should never be inveigled into any line of procedure against his deliberate judgment.

In the first place, the expectant one should frankly and unsparingly judge himself, his abilities and his inabilities. Truth is always the best friend in such matters. He must recognize the things he needs to work on in order to be the "workman that needeth not to be ashamed." He should have at least a fair English education, a working knowledge of the Bible, its chronology and major divisions, along with a sound understanding of doctrine. He needs to know something about the working of church government and history, both civil and sacred. He should have a general intelligence, sufficient to place him equal to or above those whom he is expected to serve. Certainly he cannot outstrip his congregation in all fields of learning, but in the realm of religion, truth, and morals he must be their leader. He needs to closely scrutinize his disposition and psychological concept of life in general.

How apt is the advice of Paul: "For if we would judge ourselves, we should not be judged" (I Corinthians 11:31). Then, of course, he must become a public speaker and learn to produce and deliver a sermon.

Having determined his needs, the prospective minister should prayerfully and intelligently arrive at the best procedure to follow in order to qualify himself for the ministry. It is often the case in Pentecost that its ministers are educated in the work but not out of it. Most of them learn to speak of what they feel and believe while they are seeking to know more. They, of course, do not always speak correctly or profoundly at the beginning. But in time, as they apply themselves to both work and study, they learn the art of speaking readily and forcefully. Not all who enter the ministry are privileged to attend Bible college and go through laborious and extended courses, but often their ministry is just as fruitful and productive as their more fortunate brothers.

While we cannot dictate a particular course to take in regard to entering the ministry, we must solemnly advise that every prospective minister prepare himself in view of his great responsibility to God and the immortality of souls. If God has called a person to preach, He intends that he shall succeed, and His will is for the person to shape his course accordingly. When the prospective minister senses a need in his life and realizes that he is accountable to the One who called him, he would be unwise if he did not attempt to alleviate that particular lack.

There has never been a truly great preacher who was not first a great student. "Till I come, give attendance to reading . . . meditate upon these things; give thyself wholly to them; that thy profiting may appear to all" (I Timothy 4:13-15). "Study to shew thyself approved unto God, a workman that needeth not to be ashamed, rightly dividing the word of truth" (II Timothy 2:15). Whether one enters the ministry through Bible college or not, it is imperative that he prepare himself, and this preparation involves much study. The learn-as-you-preach approach is good, but it does not preclude the need of searching, arduous study. John Wesley suggested not less than five hours of study per day for his itinerant preachers, although this practice compelled many to rise at five each morning. Preachers must understand their business in order to be successful and should not forget that God helps those who help themselves. They must pray, think, read, study, and plan to know what to say and how, when, and where to say it.

It is true that Jesus said to His first ministers, "But when they deliver you up, take no thought how or what ye shall speak: for it shall be given you in that same hour what ye shall speak" (Matthew 10:19). He did not discourage reasonable study, but He gave them comfort in view of probable surprises and emergencies when they would have no opportunity for preparation. He had already cautioned them to "beware of men" and to be as wise as serpents and harmless as doves (Matthew 10:16-17). Ministers should not worry, but rather they should help the deficiencies that they can help and work to improve themselves by all available means, so as to render themselves effective.

Let none be mistaken, the approach to the ministry is a long, hard road of prayer and study, whether in school or out, whether learning while one preaches or simply digging it out in the classroom. Regardless of which road he chooses, he should consider himself an apprentice to many truths, both practical and spiritual, until after three or four years of hard study and ministerial work. This does not mean that in this tenure the candidate cannot be winning souls, preaching, and doing much good; but in his later years, when ministerial responsibilities hem him in, he will always be glad he disciplined himself to learn basic things in those early years. To expect God to give him the requisite information without hard study on his part is fanaticism. While he is trusting Him for help and desired results, he should be just as active in seeking to be efficient as he would be if everything depended on him alone.

For the single young man called to the ministry, perhaps no better step could be taken than to settle in a Bible college for three or four years. Maturity is drastically needed. A person can engage in some fields of labor very successfully if he only knows the simple mechanics of the trade and has the ability to discharge them adequately. This is not true concerning the ministry. It is the highest of all callings, and, so long as a person's conscience will permit him, he should keep out of the ministry. Such an endeavor, laden with such tremendous significance, is not to be committed to a novice or to a nine-day wonder.

Ministerial responsibilities include the weighing of life's deepest problems and the pondering of eternal possibilities. The minister's decisions will involve small babies, wayward teenagers, and entire families. The ministry's demands escalate from kindness shown to the drunkard to invocations of the highest human order. Only the years and their accumulations can bring the poise and confidence needed for such crucial moments. While these years are passing, where can they be better spent than in school?

Youth is the golden age for education. The young person who bypasses it and dashes headlong into the ministry will sadly regret his impatience in later years. He will sense his inadequacy in a thousand ways, and scarcely a week will pass that this need of education will not glaringly present itself to him. But then it will be too late to enroll in those courses of study he foolishly disdained when he was young.

2

The Ministry in General

It is assumed that the ones who read this book are engaged in the ministry, are contemplating it, or intend to be associated with it in some close fashion. You stand on the threshold of experiences rich and real that shall intersperse all your life ahead. How wonderful that you should come into the fellowship of those who travel in such large company, and yet you must walk alone.

An early preacher on the earth was Enoch, the firstborn of Jared. (See Genesis 5:18.) Into Jared's home came a bright-eyed boy whose heart yearned after God. In Genesis 4:17 we read of another Enoch whose father was the wicked Cain. This man had a city named for him. But Genesis 5:24 says of Jared's son that "Enoch walked with God: and he was not; for God took him." Thus we see that this preacher's life was marked by his close personal relationship with God. He "walked with God." More than four thousand years later the writer to Hebrews added, "By faith

Enoch was translated that he should not see death; . . . for before his translation he had this testimony, that he pleased God" (Hebrews 11:5). This preacher had a good life and a good testimony.

He also preached the truth. Jude 14-15 records: "And Enoch also, the seventh from Adam, prophesied of these, saying, Behold, the Lord cometh with ten thousands of his saints, to execute judgment upon all, and to convince all that are ungodly among them of all their ungodly deeds which they have ungodly committed, and of all their hard speeches which ungodly sinners have spoken against him." To both preach and live the truth is the most important role that any preacher can fulfill. I wonder if the shadow of this great man's ministry is not cast sharply right at the beginning of all things, as an example to those who would later separate themselves to the same calling and follow in his steps. After Enoch there was Noah, "a preacher of righteousness." Then followed a long line of seers and prophets and finally pastors, teachers, and evangelists.

Honesty compels us to warn that the life of a minister is sprinkled not only with sunshine but shadow. Human nature in all of its complexity is certain to precipitate troubles of its own. Any minister finds the greatest part of his work, especially in the pastoral phase, in the field of human relations. Some of the problems are simple and can be taken care of with simple procedures. Others are more intricate and require foresight, tact, and patience. No one completely possesses the answer to life's tangles. It is worthy of note that a minister may make mistakes even after the most conscientious effort to be discreet. Many times a preacher of any age will chide himself and wish vainly that he had previously known the lesson that bitter experience has just taught him.

Right at the beginning of this divine adventure, we can examine a few things that will open the door just a little to what is expected in the general life of the minister.

Of course, the ministerial student is saved and feels that he has a call from God. Unless these two things are settled, there is no use going any further. The church is a spiritual organism, and it follows that no one can be effective in such a spiritual position without the feeling and leadership of the Spirit.

Principles of a Preacher's Life

The minister must love the Word of God. He should know its history and understand how it was compiled. He should, of course, know its books by heart and their authors, along with the theme and setting of each of them. He should know their groupings, the chronology of the great events in the Bible, and how the great prophecies fit into the scheme of the whole. The preacher should know Old Testament history, the Tabernacle plan, the life of Christ, the Book of Acts, and the main topics in the Epistles.

It should go without saying that the preacher must believe every word of the Bible and accept it as the very Word of God, which came directly from His divine mind and heart. None of it is to be left out, for each line and word has its particular purpose. The minister should feel in his soul the verity of the warning in Revelation 22:18-19: "If any man shall add unto these things, God shall add unto him the plagues that are written in this book: and if any man shall take away from the words of the book of this prophecy, God shall take away his part out of the book of life, and out of the holy city, and from the things which are written in this book." He must feel that God did not err in one single portion of the Bible. He must avoid questioning the authenticity of any part of the Scripture, for to do so is to weaken his own faith and the faith of those who hear him. Doubts may arise relative to people and circumstance, but at no time can the preacher afford to entertain a doubt as to the absolute truth of the Bible.

Always he must remember that it is not against flesh and blood that he wrestles, but against Satan himself. The people he deals with are not his enemies and not even his problems. For the most part, they are, in their straying, the victims of the manipulations of Satan. With this attitude, the preacher looks upon them with compassion. He feels that there is some good in all, and that in the heart of every person there is bound to be a hunger from God. It is in the outreach of compassion that the preacher endeavors to help people along the way.

In his devotions and through his observations over the years, the preacher gradually comes to see how very much God must love humans. This appreciation lends a certain respectful awe to the work of the ministry. He deals with immortal souls for whom Christ died. The work of the ministry is eternal work, for, after all material things over which people strive in this world have passed away and eternity itself has become hoary with age, the soul with which the preacher works will still be in the freshness of its youth. In the light of the eternity of human souls, what could be more rewarding than the work of the ministry?

The preacher must believe that outside of Jesus Christ

all souls are lost. If people can be saved without the Savior, there is no need to offer Him. If He is not Savior of all, then perhaps He is not the Savior at all. Feeling strongly that no one "climbeth up some other way" and that there is none other name under heaven whereby we can be saved, lends an urgency to the ministry that it would be incomplete without.

If the preacher is to help others, he must walk in the Spirit. Jesus assured us that no branch could bear fruit of itself. Invariably it must abide in the vine. "As the branch cannot bear fruit of itself, except it abide in the vine; no more can ye, except ye abide in me" (John 15:4). Nothing that the human mind alone produces or that human strength alone initiates is of any spiritual value. Only what is a direct product of the spiritual will be lasting and genuine in God's kingdom. To build with or upon anything else is sinking sand. We might have activity. We might produce something that to the unspiritual eye seems good and commendable, but to God, before whom all our works shall appear, it is but as sounding brass and a tinkling cymbal. What is born of the flesh is flesh, and what is born of the Spirit is spirit. The products of human planning and effort can be nothing more than flesh, and "no flesh should glory in his presence" (I Corinthians 1:29).

To please God, regardless of what others think, should be the highest hope of the preacher. He is to be continually vigilant so that he does not grieve the Holy Spirit. Since no one can say that Jesus Christ is Lord except by the Holy Ghost, the preacher dares not attempt to minister without the Spirit's unction. No preacher can effectively conduct a Pentecostal worship service unless he knows how to recognize the various workings of the

Spirit and is sensitive to the Spirit's leading. To woo the Holy Ghost and live under the Spirit's shadow is imperative if the preacher expects his ministry to be fruitful and lasting.

The Minister's Task

It is staggering to consider a minister's involvement in preaching the gospel and shepherding people from the time he first contacts them until loved ones finally stand beside their grave. Yet that is only one side of being a minister of the gospel. The average layperson has no way of knowing the magnitude of the preacher's responsibilities. Many feel that the minister's life is quite leisurely, with only three hours a week taken up with preaching and the rest of the time spent in hobbies and relaxation. If they are not associated closely in some way with the ministry, the laity cannot be wholly blamed for this misconception, since there is no way for them to learn differently.

There are many angles to the ministry, and each of its varied responsibilities is enough in itself to take up an average person's time. When we add them all together, without question, the scope of the ministry is large enough to challenge anyone.

No other person in the community is expected to be competent in so many diverse fields as the pastor. First and foremost, he is the leader in promoting spiritual things. No church can rise higher than its pastor in spiritual things. In this field he must not fail. Just as people visit the doctor for physical help, the congregation looks to the pastor for direction and instruction in spiritual matters. They expect him to know the way to the secret place of the Most High and to lead others there.

Because of his position, the pastor has to be the over-seer of all church departments. While others may attend to details and promotion of individual departments, it is the pastor who must know something about each and every phase of the work. All department heads must be answerable to him, and with them he must cultivate a good relationship in order to correlate the whole into a smoothly running, workable organization. He is to be the spark plug of ideas. Woe to the preacher who allows his congregation to think ahead of him! His office and keen interest in a work so dependent on him should produce plans equal to the varied needs and emergencies of the church as they arise.

The preacher finds himself the negotiator and the go-between in disputes that sometimes arise between his saints. The patience of Job and the wisdom of Solomon are coveted tools and graces of the ministry. Blessed is the minister who can perceive clearly, judge fairly, and kindly render a tactful decision. If the preacher himself becomes a part of the problem, he has disqualified him-self to mediate it. What an awkward situation it is when a pastor cannot manage his own affairs! There is no excuse he can make, for he is a specialist and is supposed to know.

The pastor is a shepherd of the flock in a closeness that is impossible to describe. It is amazing how much trust and confidence is offered to the pastors of Pentecostal churches. Surely such complete commit-ment to his care and judgment is enough to make angels hold their breath. The answer that the preacher gives had better be right, for the advice given will usually be followed. The people are the sheep who follow, and the minister is the shepherd who leads.

In the course of a year, the pastor of any sizable church is likely to see the expenditure of many thousands of dollars. As the size of the church increases, the income climbs too. Quite a few churches have incomes as great as many small businesses. The pastor heads a corporation, having under his jurisdiction department heads, sub-heads, and a host of secretaries and committees. He must know how to administrate wisely and to conduct his business affairs so that all things are proper and without shadow.

In all these things, and more, he is expected to be a specialist and not just a worker. In their given time, he must discharge each of these responsibilities well and concisely if growth and harmony is to continue. Not only must the pastor be able to teach, but he must be good enough to teach teachers how to teach. He must be able to lead leaders, build organizations, and rectify errors. He must be a student of human nature, a salesman for the gospel, and, above all, a minister of prayer and study.

Perhaps much church trouble could be avoided if the sheep were fed rightly. A layperson appreciates being able to approach the sanctuary of his home church each Sunday knowing that his pastor has labored fervently in the Word and in prayer that week and that he will hear a good Bible lesson and an inspiring sermon. After all, he is called a preacher and, though perhaps he cannot build a house or weld a pipe, no one can excuse him if he cannot preach a sermon.

A minister must be able to preside. This includes all forms of leadership. Blessed is the minister who knows how to lead his people to worship. Certainly this does not mean the ability to pump up an emotional state that leaves the participants exhausted physically and spiritually. To cause a congregation to forget their cares, their neighbors, and themselves through exalting Christ is an ability that every minister should cultivate and covet. It is pleasing if the preacher can open a service with the grace and sureness that at once puts the congregation at ease.

However, a church service is not the only place a minister will preside. The skillful hand of the pastor can guide board meetings of the church away from embarrassing circumstances. He must also preside over baptismal services, the Lord's Supper, funerals, and weddings. The average layperson is very grateful when his pastor occupies the place of attention and leadership if he is able to handle the situation forthrightly with grate and competence.

Pastoral Concern

The minister naturally carries a concern for those under his charge. The Bible speaks of the pastoral concern of the apostle Paul:

"And from Miletus he sent to Ephesus, and called the elders of the church. And when they were come to him, he said unto them, Ye know, from the first day that I came into Asia, after what manner I have been with you at all seasons, serving the Lord with all humility of mind, and with many tears, and temptations, which befell me by the lying in wait of the Jews: and how I kept back nothing that was profitable unto you, but have shewed you, and have taught you publickly, and from house to house, testifying both to the Jews, and also to the Greeks, repentance toward God,

and faith toward our Lord Jesus Christ. And now, behold, I go bound in the spirit unto Jerusalem, not knowing the things that shall befall me there: save that the Holy Ghost witnessed in every city, saying that bonds and afflictions abide me. But none of these things move me, neither count I my life dear unto myself, so that I might finish my course with joy, and the ministry, which I have received of the Lord Jesus, to testify the gospel of the grace of God. And now, behold, I know that ye all, among whom I have gone preaching the kingdom of God, shall see my face no more. Wherefore I take you to record this day, that I am pure from the blood of all men. For I have not shunned to declare unto you all the counsel of God. Take heed therefore unto yourselves, and to all the flock, over the which the Holy Ghost hath made you overseers, to feed the church of God, which he hath purchased with his own blood. For I know this, that after my departing shall grievous wolves enter in among you, not sparing the flock. Also of your own selves shall men arise, speaking perverse things, to draw away disciples after them. Therefore watch, and remember, that by the space of three years I ceased not to warn every one night and day with tears. And now, brethren, I commend you to God, and to the word of his grace, which is able to build you up, and to give you an inheritance among all them which are sanctified" (Acts 20:17-32).

There is nowhere in the Bible, or out of it, a more touching example of the care a pastor should have for his flock.

The minister's work is not dependent upon his natural ability. The apostle Paul explained:

"And I, brethren, when I came to you, came not with excellency of speech or of wisdom, declaring unto you the testimony of God. For I determined not to know any thing among you, save Jesus Christ, and him crucified. And I was with you in weakness, and in fear, and in much trembling. And my speech and my preaching was not with enticing words of man's wisdom, but in demonstration of the Spirit and of power: that your faith should not stand in the wisdom of men, but in the power of God" (I Corinthians 2:1-5).

Paul could have used great, swelling words. He could have interested them with mysterious lessons and strange utterances. He could have thus gathered to himself a great company of admiring followers. But he knew that in gathering them to himself, he would not have gathered them to Christ. The ability of a person is not sufficient to produce the smallest outcropping of Christian life. The reason that Paul hid his abilities in weakness and trembling is revealed in the last clause of the quoted passage of Scripture: "that your faith should not stand in the wisdom of men, but in the power of God" (I Corinthians 2:5).

The minister is among the people as a servant.

"For though I be free from all men, yet have I made myself servant unto all, that I might gain the more. And unto the Jews I became as a Jew, that I might gain the Jews; to them that are under the law, as under the law,

33

that I might gain them that are under the law; to them that are without law, as without law, (being not without law to God, but under the law to Christ,) that I might gain them that are without law. To the weak became I as weak, that I might gain the weak: I am made all things to all men, that I might by all means save some. And this I do for the gospel's sake, that I might be partaker thereof with you" (I Corinthians 9:19-23).

Here it seems that human preference must have been almost completely rubbed out of the apostle in his strenuous effort to save others. He adapted himself, spent himself, and made himself a "servant unto all."

A Lonely Life

The life of a minister is often lonely and fraught with trials:

"Giving no offence in any thing, that the ministry be not blamed: but in all things approving ourselves as the ministers of God, in much patience, in afflictions, in necessities, in distresses, in stripes, in imprisonments, in tumults, in labours, in watchings, in fastings; by pureness, by knowledge, by longsuffering, by kindness, by the Holy Ghost, by love unfeigned, by the word of truth, by the power of God, by the armour of righteousness on the right hand and on the left, by honour and dishonour, by evil report and good report: as deceivers, and yet true; as unknown, and yet well known; as dying, and, behold, we live; as chastened, and not killed; as sorrowful, yet always rejoicing; as poor, yet making many rich; as having

nothing, and yet possessing all things" (II Corinthians 6:3-10).

There are times when a preacher must walk absolutely alone, not heeding the advice of even his wife, not being able to disclose to his closest friends the burden that crushes his heart. To be a leader is always to be lonely, but when one is a leader in spiritual things, the loneliness seems to be multiplied a hundredfold. For it is impossible for a preacher to heal the needs that he does not feel. If the shortcomings of his congregation are not as a knife in his own heart, it is very likely that he can never come to the real crux of the matter.

The qualifications of a minister strongly involve his personal life:

"This is a true saying, If a man desire the office of a bishop, he desireth a good work. A bishop then must be blameless, the husband of one wife, vigilant, sober, of good behaviour; given to hospitality, apt to teach; not given to wine, no striker; not greedy of filthy lucre; but patient, not a brawler; not covetous; one that ruleth well his own house, having his children in subjection with all gravity; (for if a man know not how to rule his own house, how shall he take care of the church of God?) not a novice, lest being lifted up with pride he fall into the condemnation of the devil. Moreover he must have a good report of them which are without; lest he fall into reproach and the snare of the devil" (I Timothy 3:1-7).

These words touch almost every avenue of a preacher's life, from being "blameless" to being a good family man and taking care of his own life. These are personal qualifications that he is expected to live up to, "for if a man know not how to rule his own house [or life], how shall he take care of the church of God?" Sometimes the minister's greatest battlefield is the arena of his own soul, where conscience sits down with human weakness and with righteousness. There eternal issues are decided that might involve even the preacher's ultimate destiny. We should note the warning of Paul to the young preacher, Timothy: "But thou, O man of God, flee these things; and follow after righteousness, godliness, faith, love, patience, meekness. Fight the good fight of faith, lay hold on eternal life, whereunto thou art also called, and hast professed a good profession before many witnesses" (I Timothy 6:11-12).

Happy is the minister who can make a graceful exit. The prayer of Solomon was that he might know how to go out and to come in before the people. Once there was an actor who did a superb job of acting, but when his marvelous act was over and he prepared to exit amid thunderous applause, he slipped and fell. To say the least, his exit was not with grace. We cannot help but think of the goodbye of the soldier Paul:

"I charge thee therefore before God, and the Lord Jesus Christ, who shall judge the quick and the dead at his appearing and his kingdom; preach the word; be instant in season, out of season; reprove, rebuke, exhort with all longsuffering and doctrine. For the time will come when they will not endure sound doctrine; but after their own lusts shall they heap to themselves teachers, having itching ears; and they shall turn away their

ears from the truth, and shall be turned unto fables. But watch thou in all things, endure afflictions, do the work of an evangelist, make full proof of thy ministry. For I am now ready to be offered, and the time of my departure is at hand. I have fought a good fight, I have finished my course, I have kept the faith" (II Timothy 4:1-7).

What more gracious words could be said at life's closing day? A few hours before the late W. T. Witherspoon died, he asked to be propped up in bed and there, leaning weakly back on the pillows, he declared, "It is not the messenger that is important, it is the message that he carries. The messenger must perish, but the message will go on."

He who wants to preach had better tremble when he says it—tremble for the glory of the battle and tremble for the demand of the task.

3

The Minister As a Person

The life a preacher lives through the week has a strange way of following him into the pulpit each Sunday. It is impossible for a preacher to separate his ministry from himself. The mechanic may clean his tools, put them in their box, lock it, and go home for the weekend. His tools remain outside of himself, and on the weekend he can cast himself in a role other than that of a mechanic. His tools do not follow him on his excursions. It is different with the preacher. He himself, his emotions, his convictions, and his reactions are his tools.

Thus the minister's reputation is first scrutinized before his work is accepted. The craftsman examines his tool before starting his work. In like manner the preacher, as a person, must live on the scales of judgment—his own introspection and the scrutiny of the public as well. In all other fields and professions the worker is able to divorce himself, at least in part, from the tools and demands of his trade, but with the preacher it is not so. He is the tool, and the tool cannot run away from itself. His sermons and all his work are invariably colored by the honor or dishonor of the person himself. It is impossible for his work, however well executed, to rise higher than the repute of the producer.

The goldfish bowl of his public life allows him no private seclusion where the venom of his worse self can be dissipated in private, hid forever from the knowledge of his congregation. Sin always finds the preacher out, more so, it seems, than anyone else. And if sin could be hidden, its stains would be upon the preacher's heart and soul. Thus even hidden sins effect their retributive work on the preacher, for his heart, soul and emotions are the tools of his trade. When cankered by deceit and rusted by sin, the work is sure to be faulty. The preacher is an "epistle . . . known and read of all men" (II Corinthians 3:2). He cannot promote a spiritual good that is beyond his present experience.

This being true, the preacher must spend some part of his time looking at himself. All tools must be well-kept, clean, and sharp if they are to produce vessels of honor in the Lord's house. Let us examine some of the qualities that must reside in the life of a minister if he is to be complete, lacking in nothing.

Physical Strength

The minister should be physically strong. Mysteriously, a church pastored for some length of time by one person has a way of assuming some of the traits of the pastor's personality. The aggressive person of decisive action seems to project this same robustness into the life of the church. This being so, for the sake of his charge, the preacher should attempt to stay healthy. Since his service and preaching are in part products of his physical body, his health will obviously have a bearing on them.

A doctor once confided concerning a good preacher who passed away after surgery, "I know the reverend would not have thought of taking a drink of whiskey, but by his habit of overeating he has done the same thing that whiskey would have done to some of his organs." This should not be. For a great and good ministry to come to an end at age fifty or before, because of a physical breakdown, is such a waste.

The ministry is a job for strong people. The muscles are not those of a log roller, of course, but by nature of his service, the stamina and endurance of a Pentecostal preacher must be good. The Pentecostal ministry is no place for effeminate men. In having conferences or camp meetings, once in a while we will shake a hand with calluses and tough fingernails. Let it be so now and always among God's people!

However, there are others who, while not strong in body, are doubly strong in spirit and seem to do the work of ten. May such traits never fade from the ranks of Pentecost.

The pastor and evangelist should, without condemnation from themselves or others, take their vacations each year and have one day a week off. The minister, because of the nature of his work, cannot always be specific in which day he takes off. Were it not that church business, plus the sick discovered on Sunday, often has to be taken care of on Monday, that would be an ideal day of rest.

41

Monday night is preferred by many for a rest night during special services, since it gives schoolchildren rest on a school night. Inasmuch as Saturday anticipates the strain of Sunday, it provides little rest.

In whatever relaxation the preacher engages, it should be different from his routine work. Because of interruptions, it is better for him to get out of town if possible. A person who has as wide a circle of friends and acquaintances as a minister is subject to calls or visits on any day.

Some ministers enjoy hunting or fishing, while others are able to unwind completely with a short trip, a drive in the country, a picnic with the family, or merely puttering about the yard or house. Humans are so made that they usually come to a normal emotional level quicker through employment of their hands and in doing something they enjoy than in any other way.

Perhaps few people, including the preacher himself, realize the beating that he gives his body over the process of twenty years of active ministry. For the Pentecostal preacher, the loss of sleep over a period of possibly weeks is a factor in undermining his health. Fortunately, this situation is not usually continuous and, according to scientific findings, physical stamina snaps back as soon as more sleep is available.

The conscientious, productive pastor who continually fills his pulpit, in addition to teaching each Sunday, will do almost as much creative work as the editor of a small newspaper. Then we must add to sermon building the administrative side of the church, plus pastoral problems and the mental load. This pouring out of mental creations, ideas, and important decisions wrings considerable strength from a person.

But the greatest toll taken on a minister is in the area of emotions. He lavishly expends nervous energy in almost every department of ministerial responsibility. There is an invariable anxiety attached to pastoral counseling, to say nothing of other involvements that embrace the entire church structure. Like Christ, the undershepherd is touched continuously by the feelings and needs of others, each being as near as his telephone. Unlike the worker who punches the clock and walks off the job, leaving all its problems behind, the pastor is on call twenty-four hours. While he walks the streets of his community, he is not relaxed. For the sake of his church and charge, he must speak and be friendly to all at every opportunity.

This being true, not only is it important for him to participate once a week in a relaxing diversion, but he should also engage in some form of physical exercise every day. He can get some exercise in the normal process of each day if he is alert to the opportunities. He should break the habit of looking for a parking place nearest the door of the hospital or any other place. He should gladly take each chance to walk whenever possible. A brisk walk at top speed will do wonders to stretch the flabby leg muscles and make the sluggish heart pound. Deliberately parking the car a block or so away from his destination becomes a good health aide. Stairs are a preacher's friend. He should never shun them for an elevator unless he is aged or physically impaired. Many busy people make it a point, for health's sake, never to ride an elevator.

Besides what little exercise can be gathered through the day, there is nothing more refreshing than ten minutes of calisthenics immediately after rising, followed by a good shower. Exercise helps muscle tone, aids circulation, brings a sense of well-being, and makes the brain sharp and keen for the day. Otherwise, precious hours are lost during a week due to slow starts in the morning, perpetuated by a foggy brain and a slow heartbeat.

There is not one scale, of course, by which to judge all to determine if they are in shape physically. The physical needs of the basketball player are quite different from those of a preacher. Hence, if a person is physically able to energetically discharge his responsibilities in his given field of labor without undue fatigue or effort, and his weight, muscle tone, and other pertinent factors are in good order, then he is well on his way to being physically fit.

A Good, Strong Attitude

It is not the work that breaks the preacher but his approach and attitude toward it. If he labors indefinitely under inhibitions of fear and uncertainty, he is sure of an adverse physical reaction. Blessed is the person who learns early that the flesh cannot effect a spiritual work in the church. In fact, in the final analysis, there is little that any preacher does. The lasting good is done by God, while the minister plods along, adding his little bit. It is a golden day for the pastor when he discovers that all God asks of him is not his achievement but his faithfulness. If a person faithfully discharges his duty in love and wisdom and things still go to pieces, he can comfort himself in that the situation would likely have occurred no matter who was in charge. All God expects of anyone is to do his best. It is God's church, and if He cannot fix a problem, what can a mortal do anyway? So long as a minister can sleep well, work relaxed, and trust God for what he cannot help, there is almost no end to the amount of work he can bear.

A preacher can be ruined by self-pity. He begins to imagine that, of all people, he is the most overworked. The truth is that the average Pentecostal preacher carries hardly half the load of any leading surgeon in his town. There should be no room for self-pity even in the lives of the most ill-used. Self-pity saps courage, causes atrophy of the nerve, and is the cancer of the will. Self-pity can be a person's worst enemy, and he must not give place to it— not for the space of one hour. If necessary, he should speak sternly and unsparingly to himself, or ask another to do it for him.

Since proper emotion is a part of a minister's stock in trade, he ought to cultivate it. To be effective he must, in some measure, wear the right feelings on his sleeve. Jeremiah, David, Peter, and Paul were all men of emotion and tears. However, the minister can tend toward morbidity if he does not frequently count the many blessings that Christ sends.

It is easy to be spoiled. A minister may receive various benefits and hardly stop to be grateful. He may expect discounts at stores and for professional services. Often church members are expected to share their commissions. He may expect a preferred standing in just about all things and become irritated if it is not forthcoming.

The preacher who hits the self-pity slide is usually headed for a breakdown. Annas and Caiaphas in the days of Jesus, not to mention the priests of the Middle Ages, expected preferred treatment, and their religion died in their hands. The cloak of the ministry does not hide the pettiness that is often the progenitor of self-pity. Real ministers do not want pity; they only ask for understanding and a chance to try again.

A teacher in a certain school consistently had discipline problems, so much that her resignation was finally requested. Her trouble was not that she did not know her text, the techniques of presenting it, or her responsibilities. She simply could not keep order and hold command of her class. Through the years she had been unable to discipline herself. No one can lead others where he himself has not been led.

How great the compliment Jesus gave to the man who had emptied all Judah into the Jordan River bottoms! "What went ye out into the wilderness to see? A reed shaken in the wind? But what went ye out for to see? A man clothed in soft raiment? behold, they that wear soft clothing are in kings' houses. But what went ye out for to see? A prophet? yea, I say unto you, and more than a prophet. For this is he, of whom it is written, Behold, I send my messenger before thy face, which shall prepare thy way before thee. Verily I say unto you, Among them that are born of women there hath not risen a greater than John the Baptist" (Matthew 11:7-11).

Humility

One of the greatest virtues that a minister can be graced with is humility. True humility does not come as a person strives for it, but it is a byproduct that is always present when other virtues have their rightful place in the life of a preacher. Humility is not thinking meanly of oneself but simply not thinking of oneself at all and allowing self to be swallowed up in an ideal or cause far more important. It is not as necessary for the preacher to keep his finger on his spiritual pulse as it is for him to forget himself in loving God and others. He needs to be challenged from the outside as soldiers are challenged on the field or surgeons are in the operating room, when they are asked for their very best.

Flattery is the enemy of humility, and every preacher, whether great or small, gets far more of it than is good for him. After his sermon, whether it was good, bad or indifferent, people will come by and pass along some kind remark concerning it. This does not happen just on special occasions, or even only on Sunday, but the average Pentecostal preacher receives compliments quite often. If a preacher can listen to them all his life without coming to believe them, he has an unusually level head. Most human beings are affected by flattery far more than they realize. Mere constant reiteration has its effect. If, on any particular occasion, the praise does not happen to be lavished, the vain one will feel neglected, though he will probably refuse to acknowledge this even to himself. Vaguely in the sky a cloud hangs, making the rest of Sunday or Monday gloomy and cold.

Kind Pentecostal people who love the ministry are neither insincere nor intentional flatterers. Perhaps some of them did not understand what the sermon was about. Their compliments were meant as a tribute to the position the shepherd holds among them and as an encouragement in what he is trying to do. These good people are for the minister in the same way the minister is for them, and they believe in the thing he is trying to do. Thus each Sunday they leave their personal endorsement. The entire service meant something to them, their best nature was appealed to by Christian worship, and it is only natural that they express this to their leader. They are perfectly sincere, but they are much more impersonal than a minister's vanity likes to realize, and there is not as much cause to let his chest expand as he too often thinks.

Most people in other walks of life are not subjected to this temptation, at least not in the same degree. When a doctor cures a patient, everyone is glad, but there is no line of admirers outside the sick room to tell him how wonderful he is. The lawyer does not expect popular acclaim for every suit he argues, and the businessman is as apt to be criticized as to be praised for a successful business deal. It is no wonder that the preacher is often grossly deceived in his estimate of himself and his ability.

In every congregation there are several people who can be counted on to come to church in a spirit of prayer and who are saintly enough to find good in everything, including the sermon, regardless of how poor it might have been. They can be counted on to find something helpful in it and to tell the preacher so. Everyone else, out of respect, did not criticize the message, so a gullible preacher, by a unanimous vote of three to nothing, assumes that it must have been great. Since a self-conceited person is so obvious and so disgusting, how important it is that the minister have the right conception of himself and be clothed with humility! Great preachers are always made out of humble people.

Faithfulness

The preacher must be faithful. "A bishop then must be blameless" (I Timothy 3:2). As there are no fixed stan-

48

dards in this profession, a minister must be all the more introspective. Laziness has often been called the preacher's besetting sin. There is no fixed time to report for work in the morning, no limited lunch hours, no whistle for knocking off in the afternoon, so it is a moral test for a preacher to be in entire control of his time.

Any of the varied and multiple demands made upon a minister is enough to consume all of his time. Preaching, pastoring, soulwinning, administration, and denominational activities, taken separately, are each fields of their own and capable of consuming all of one's time. Unfaithfulness in any of them will react adversely on a church's progress. None of these can be slighted by a preacher without his dereliction catching up with him in various forms of trouble. The long, hard hours of study necessary for fresh preaching, the dedication to the sick and struggling, the aggressive outreach necessary to enlist and win the lost will never be assumed by a selfish, ease-loving, lazy preacher. Only a sanctified dedication to sacred duty will perpetually drive a preacher forward into his field of labor. If he does not love God and his call, and if he has not at some point in his life learned the discipline of good stewardship, he will not keep going.

The lazy preacher has many loopholes in his profession through which he can escape if he so desires. The very nature of his work assures that he could be doing good almost anywhere and at any time of the day. If he is at home, he could be studying. It is easy to answer the door with a book or Bible in hand. If he is driving the streets, it is easy to say he has been visiting, though he may have made only one call. Even a trip out of town can be justified. Only God and the preacher know if he is a dedicated worker or a lazy hypocrite. Laziness is not appreciated in anyone, but how impossible it is to describe the contempt people feel for a lazy preacher! A person cannot leave most of the church work for his wife, never turning his hand about the house, sleeping late, and letting things go to rot in general, without the congregation knowing. Often such a preacher, strangely, cannot understand why his parishioners turn away from him in disgust and why his time is largely spent looking for another place to go.

This lack of ministerial standards applies in many ways. There is not a clear system of measurement to tell him if he is succeeding or failing. The doctor either cures his patient or does not, and if he fails habitually, the cemetery stands as mute evidence of his inefficiency. The lawyer either wins his case or loses it, and the judge or jury passes judgment. But preachers have no automatic measurements, and any that is accepted may be misleading. We have already mentioned the folly of using compliments from the congregation as evidence of success. Often success is measured by the ability to care for the interest of the church by raising money, building buildings, and increasing Sunday school attendance. But who can know the quality of holiness in the hearts of the congregation? Thus, of all people, the preacher is upon his own honor and is trusted to do a good job. Such being so, how black is discrepancy in matters where faithfulness is so expected!

A strong leader must be an optimist. This does not mean that he should deviate from facts as they are and eternally gloss over glaring possibilities of danger or trouble, but maturity and close fellowship with God cast out fear. A whimpering and whining preacher seldom does much for Christ. If discouragement is the lot of the pastor, he is wise to hide it from the church. If he will only look, he can always find something before the next service to encourage him in the Lord. Taking all into consideration, there is really little to hinder a man of God from being a buoyant and happy Christian. At any rate, if a pastor hopes to shepherd a happy, joyous congregation, he must be their example.

People expect the minister to be strong enough for them to lean on and to help them bear their burdens. After all, this is why he is their leader. Everyone has his misfortunes and trials and is often reluctant to listen to the troubles of a preacher. Sometimes there is no layperson in any congregation capable of helping a preacher with his problem. He must often look to God, and God alone, for his encouragement.

Honesty

Of all virtues, a minister should strive to add honesty to his life. In most things the average Pentecostal preacher will be conscientiously honest, but there can be a lurking, subtle dishonesty that is the bane of the pulpit.

There are many ways to dilute the truth. The preacher can glibly and falsely state the approximate number who are absent on a Sunday evening. Swept up in the fervor of his message, his heart yearning to persuade his congregation, the earnest preacher can, without premeditation, begin to stretch facts. But untruthfulness cannot be justified by a motive of furthering the kingdom of God. Besides the harm done to a discerning audience, the loss that the preacher incurs in his own soul by such misrepresentation of facts is enough to cause him to be very careful.

Great and outlandish moral sins that shame and curse the ministry and church, without a doubt have their beginning in the preacher's being untrue to his better self in smaller matters. A preacher should not, under any circumstances, be a liar. Fabricating illustrations and passing them off as experiences, when they never happened, is misleading. The preacher must know that neither the Bible, God, nor one's conscience will justify his telling a lie, no matter what circumstance nor how lofty the apparent motive might be.

When a preacher gives his word, he should regard it as a sacred bond. If he makes an appointment, he should expend every effort to keep that appointment and to be there on time. If the minister sees that he is to be late, he should call at once and let the waiting party know.

Letters of recommendation for jobs, letters of membership transfer, and recommendations to churches for preacher friends can all be pitfalls for dishonesty. A minister must always be truthful.

Patience

Patience is a grace that must be a part of the ministry, for without it the preacher will not possess, for long, either his soul or his church. In the close community of church life, many small irritants can easily develop. Under the pressure of important occasions and time limitations, it is easy to reveal an impatient spirit. Pressure reveals the true person. A minister is simply expected to remain calm and collected under trying circumstances. He cannot blow his top many times without losing his lid altogether. In time, prayer and the daily presence of Jesus will help the preacher to overcome common tribulations of the ministry and develop a sturdy, patient personality.

In the flesh, Jesus was not able to meet all the people's needs in the many villages and towns of Palestine. Beyond lay the far-flung boundaries of the Roman Empire, lost to the uttermost. The people about Him were carnal and lacking in spiritual perception, craving only what appealed to their materialistic greed. The crowds, hot and sweaty, pushed against Him. After He healed one sick person before Him, He knew there would be another and then another until the day's end would drive them home. Tomorrow would be another day, and there were other towns; it was like the continual lifting of a stone that ever must be lifted again. Finally, beyond it all waited the Cross. Such was the lot of Christ, and yet He ever remained patient. "He was moved with compassion on them." (See Matthew 9:36.)

Compassion breeds patience. Love engenders the tenderness and helpfulness that often need to be extended again and again. The minister who does not love people in all their limitations had better find a more compatible vocation, for people who are not covered by love can be a very disappointing stock in trade.

Money Management

The existence of a ditch on both sides of the road is nowhere more acutely real than in the realm of a minister's financial management. A good minister can have an income so small that he is forced to frugality in order to live within his means and is in danger of being labeled a tightwad. It is bad when a preacher, because of financial expediency, is forced to act as though he has fishhooks in his pocket when the bill comes at a restaurant. He, as anyone, should be able to carry his share of a common bill. By virtue of his influence, a stingy preacher can in time kill the liberality of a congregation. The other side of the picture is that of a money grabber and money waster. Between the two extremes a preacher must find a compatible position and stick to it.

The minister should be one of the sharpest buyers in town, yet not using his office for personal gain. If a discount is offered on a given item, it should be graciously accepted, followed later by a mailed note of thanks.

Sometimes it is unethical to ask for a ministerial discount. The feeling of many business owners is that the preacher is paid for his services by the people he serves, the same as any other professional. Inasmuch as discounts are not given to doctors or lawyers, why should the preacher expect them? There is no question that resentment is often felt when it is known that a well-paid minister expects the commission and profit to be shared with him. Peace in a church and the goodwill of the people are of far more value than a new car or extra-fine cloth.

Adjusting his standard of living to his income is a must for the preacher. He must discipline himself to live without many things that he would like, if he cannot actually or ethically afford them. A standard of living that is above what a church is really able to afford is not only unfair to the church but to the pastor's family as well. Who can determine where any of God's servants will be one year from now? It is hard to step down to less pay after one is used to lavish spending.

Impulse buying can squeeze a person into financial straits. Clutters of unneeded and unused items about a preacher's garage and home indicate immaturity in judgment relative to spending. No preacher can afford to waste money in this fashion. This money could be set aside to purchase insurance or some form of annuity for the coming day when his earning power is expended. The minister with ample income now is morally responsible to provide for the sunset years of his life.

Who doubts the unfairness of foolish spending now by one who will later become a financial liability to society? The trait of providing for one's own and of being able to stand alone because of sound money management is a trait any congregation appreciates in its pastor.

Many a person has been ruined financially by overindulgence in installment buying. It is not necessary to say that a preacher should never establish a credit account or buy anything on the installment plan. Many, today, would have little or nothing if this provision were not accessible. Yet it is easy to overindulge, and preachers are not invulnerable at this point.

However, to become too money conscious is to lose the effectiveness of a ministry. The waters become muddied, the stream polluted, and soon the congregation sickens over the love of filthy lucre infesting the ministry. It is said that when, for money's sake, an artist begins to paint canvas by the yard, he is through as a promising person in his field. His interest has been diverted from his first love to something that is not art at all, but greed. The same is true and more so of the minister.

Civic Life

The prophet must conduct with care his association in the civic life of his community. There was a time when the minister was regarded much more highly than he is today. He was looked up to as one set apart. Conversation was kept on the highest plane while he was present. However, this is not altogether so today.

A contributing factor in this decline of respect is the laxity of ministers of various denominations in social conduct and association. Very few clubs and civic organizations in a town can offer fellowship on the ministerial level. To be sure, they welcome and encourage the membership of a preacher, but sooner or later something will be offered that the man of God cannot, for conscience' sake, condone. Embarrassment will inevitably shame him back to what God has called him to do.

If a preacher gave his ear, time, and pulpit to every suggestion and need of civic work, the preaching of the gospel would be left out. He should choose discreetly this better part and determine that it shall not be taken from him.

One wonders why the organizers of various functions think it so necessary for a preacher to bless those functions with prayer. Such a desire is not altogether an indication of Christianity but more of a ritualistic, formal procedure that smacks of paganism. There are some things that God's man cannot ask God to bless.

The preacher must be true to his convictions and to his better self, and he should not cheapen his position by offering a prayer that cannot, because of the nature of the case, be sincere. Hollow mockery, either in life or in prayer, has no place in the ministry.

4

The Preacher and His Home

Some time ago, a great corporation in one of the southern states reached a certain conclusion concerning the various troubles that afflicted their personnel. Their employees' efficiency was known to fall off appreciably under the stress of these problems. The company concluded that the two most efficiency-wrecking problems that could befall a person were family trouble and church trouble. If this be true in secular employment, it is doubly so regarding the ministry.

The preacher cannot preach as freely, nor administer as wisely, when his heart is being eaten out by a cancerous maladjustment in his home. Preaching is strong in its emotional factor. If the springs that give rise to the holy persuasions of the pulpit are to be strong and healthy, they must not be muddied by the splashing feet of willful and hurtful behavior in the home. Personality clashes in the parsonage during the week can quickly drain away the power reserves so sorely needed for Sunday morning and Sunday night.

Unhealthy family relations can horribly blunt the calm and keen insight that enables a minister to cut across the irrelevancies and arrive quickly at the heart of church problems. It is essential for the pastor's judgment to be objective and unprejudiced. Searing and jolting experiences in his own home can warp his judgment and make him impatient with the problem of another.

While other professionals might, with some degree of success, leave their troubles behind the front door of their home when they sally forth to meet the day, the preacher's home life has a strange way of coming to church with him. It sits on the pew right before him and listens to him preach. It verifies or repudiates every sermon, adding strength to it or mercilessly subtracting from its effectiveness. There is no other profession in which a person's success is so dependent on his family. Since this is true, we must not minimize or ignore the care and consideration that the preacher should give to family ties.

The Minister's Spouse

As no other employer, the church has to associate itself with the minister's spouse. Perhaps the question most often put to sectional presbyters and district superintendents by church boards seeking a new pastor is "What kind of wife does he have?" It is in the ministry that men are most likely to be made or broken by their wives.

To serve God at his best, the minister must have married the proper kind of girl. If she is lazy, his study habits will become haphazard. He will wash dishes and care for children instead of getting his sermons, and his pulpit work will lose its luster. If she lacks sympathy or is selfish, the unending demands of the pastorate and the everrecurring heartaches of the church members will irk her and then irritate him. If she is unconsecrated and dull of spiritual vision she will become critical and at last be a plain hindrance to the work of her husband.

In contrast, a holy, kind, God-loving minister's wife whose life complements her husband in every point can inspire an ordinary husband to become an extraordinary leader in the work of Christ. Such a woman takes her biblical place as a helper to her husband, capable of maintaining a supporting role without envy. Her ability to absorb shocks without being dismayed, to meet sorrow bravely, and to grow in grace and discipline will call forth the best from her pastor husband. So important is she to the minister, to their children, and to their service that the pastor's vision, unselfishness, zest for God, and total worth to His kingdom depend to a great extent on the wife and mother of the parsonage family.

Such a woman is not entirely self-made. She, as everyone, is more or less a product of her environment. A young minister looking for a wife should consider her background as well as the immediate quality of her consecration and spiritual interest. If she does not, in mature youth, manifest some semblance of these characteristics, it is foolish to presume that she will develop them later.

However, it is certainly unfair to expect of a young wife who has just moved into her first parsonage the confidence, poise, and knowledge that come with years of ministerial association. It is distinctly advantageous that most young preachers and their wives have a chance to grow up together. The wife will never need to know as much as her preacher husband. It is hoped that he did not marry her as an institution but as a companion, life partner, and homemaker.

A preacher should be careful not to expect too much from his wife as an individual. A wife is, first, a human being and not a traditional institution designed according to orthodox specifications. A minister who makes his wife happy will do it as a human being, and he will make it personal. The ministry is a demanding, time-consuming, energy-burning profession. The minister needs to pray for himself as a husband. There is no doubt of the unfairness of a preacher's bringing back to his wife, day after day, only shreds of personal interest, response, joy, laughter, and concern—the bulk of the man she married having been poured out freely into the lives of the church membership. It is too much to expect the wife to supply daily the joy, interest, and concern for family solidarity while the preacher husband presents only a passive, inert body and possibly an uninterested grunt occasionally from behind the newspaper.

It is surprising, but true, that most women who have married preachers did not have the ministry as their first interest. Perhaps they had been interested in God's work generally and, as good Christians, had a love for God, but as women their first interest was in their husbands as men and not a profession. The psychology of a woman is bound up in courtship, marriage, and children. These are very personal and intimate matters, and they reflect the feminine expectation in the married life.

A woman cannot be taken for granted for a long time and remain happy. She must be noticed and appreciated for herself. Her future is secure because her husband was attracted to her personally, so much that he promised before God and witnesses that he would always care for her material and emotional needs. Her sense of well-being and security is enhanced throughout the marriage as long as she feels that her husband is still attracted to her in a warm and personal way. She looks for the manifestation of this attraction in the interest that her husband shows in her household accomplishments, the events of her day, her new hairdo, and many small things.

A wife will never be happy merely succeeding as a pastor's wife. That is too cold and remote for any woman. She must feel that she is succeeding as a man's wife, and this she can believe only when he is aware of her in a personal way. Subconsciously, she feels that her livelihood, her material and emotional needs are assured only on the basis of her husband's personal acceptance of her, and she must continually receive this assurance if she is to remain happy. To suppose that she should be satisfied with promises made at the marriage altar and statements of love and fidelity pronounced in early marriage, is to expect too much of a wife. This is expecting her to be something other than a woman, and this she can never successfully be and, at the same time, remain as he would want her.

An ideal wife is a product, at least in part, of the man she married. It is the privilege of a man to cultivate the best side of his wife's nature and to help her overcome the weaker side. Often the worst side of a wife's personality is thrown up in defense against her husband's impatience, irritability, and lack of understanding. Over the years, this will cause sweet, even-tempered girls to unintentionally learn the art of striking back, pouting, and sour silence.

A pastor's wife has the right to expect from her husband the same courtesy and kindness that he would show any woman of his congregation. But too often she, from day to day, sees her husband at his worst. She is well acquainted with his tiredness, discouragement, impatience, and irritability. Sometimes it seems that all the kindness and sweetness of his character dissipates when he parks his car in the garage and enters the company of the only one before whom he does not have to act his best.

The children must also be considered in this regard. It is not right that those innocent ones who did not ask to be born into a preacher's home, and have no call to preach, should receive nothing from the parsonage head but frowns, corrections, and irritability.

It is safe to say that most often the fault of marital unhappiness in the parsonage lies at the feet of the preacher.

The minister should not expect his wife to cease from being a woman, with a woman's personality and a woman's needs. An inward conflict over their role accounts for some of the nervous breakdowns that some preachers' wives have experienced. Complexes created by personal neglect have caused some women to cease functioning in the marital role of a true wife.

The mantle of the ministry does not guarantee happiness in the Pentecostal church parsonage. Happiness comes with a price tag, and the price must be paid.

It is a good idea for the preacher to set aside some time to enjoy his wife's company and allow nothing to violate it. At times they should leave the children with others so that, for a carefree afternoon, the pastor may simply be a man in the company of his wife. A little window-shopping trip, lunch together, or a trip alone out of town can mean so much in creating and furthering mutual understanding between husband and wife. How subtly and insidiously will duty and time steal away the strength and solidarity of a marriage bond!

No home is stronger than the unity of its first relation, which is the union of husband and wife. Around this first unit the family assembles, and their strength is determined by the strength of it. The effects of the relationships in the parsonage spread out like ripples in a pond to the uttermost circumference of the preacher's ministry, verifying and lifting or contradicting and blighting.

A preacher is expecting too much of his wife if he allows her to be burdened down with an overload of church responsibility. By experience and ability, the minister's wife typically makes herself susceptible to many and varied church responsibilities. These are piled upon her willing shoulders until there is hardly time left for the poor woman to live. Seeing in his wife one of his greatest assets, a wise preacher will not allow the church to take undue advantage of her. Not only does he love her, but sound judgment tells him that once her health is broken, she cannot help him at all.

He must also consider that his children need their mother. Since the children receive more care from their mother in early life and for years eat food prepared primarily by her hands, they tend to lean strongly toward their mother. When the woman is continually taken out of the parsonage by church responsibilities, so that the children are left to themselves, a backlog of trouble can result, canceling out all the good that she is attempting.

In new churches and struggling works where the

ladies do much of the work of the church, including fund raising, there often seems to be no choice. In this situation the preacher's wife takes a beating and often bears a far heavier load than her husband. Especially is this true if the pastor is not doing any secular work.

The same woman has a home to care for, cooking to do, and the children and a husband to minister to. No doubt she also leads the ladies prayer group and teaches a Sunday school class. A considerate husband will recognize his wife's stress and, as soon as possible, take steps to relieve it. He knows the loss of his wife would be impossible to calculate; and it is better for his children's sake, her sake, and the sake of his ministry to go slower, that she might be able to work more effectively and for a longer time.

The secret of good leadership is the ability to develop leadership in others and to delegate it effectively. While some departments of the church can most effectively be administered by the pastor's wife, others could just as well be supervised by a gifted layperson. Leadership is not determined in how much a leader does, but in how much he is able to motivate and organize others to do.

Of all homes in the city, none deserves the convenience of modern appliances more than the parsonage. Anything that a preacher can afford to buy, anything that he can do to make his wife's load lighter, so that she might have more time with their children, is advisable. In years to come, other preachers will be preaching in the pulpits he once preached in, other pastors will be caring for the people he ministered to as his own, and all that he will have left is his family and the qualities he has built into their lives. If he has not been a husband deserving of his wife's respect and love, he may rest assured that he will not have it at a time he wants and needs it the most.

A home and family is an investment. Through the years, the wise preacher deposits every day into this institution companionship, love and mutual understanding. When his active ministry is over, he will need what he so freely gave in his strength to come back to him in the days of his weakness. The aged preacher who provided not for his own household may wait and listen in vain for the tender caress and the soft word of kindness from those he neglected in his busy years.

If too much is expected of the preacher's wife, all the high sense of duty to God and the church will sometimes not keep resentment from smothering tender feelings toward the man who allowed it to happen. It is the husband's place to guard his wife's welfare and look after her as tenderly after marriage as he was thoughtful of her before.

The Minister's Children

The preacher also has duties toward his children. The very professional difference of the minister's home accents the need that children have for close fellowship with their parents. Parsonage life seems to develop an affinity for family devotion and loyalty. Perhaps this is one of the reasons it hurts so badly when there is conflict.

A parsonage child who feels he has a real grievance usually feels helpless to do much about it. He is hemmed in by loyalty to his father's position and by what is expected from him by the congregation. Often he develops more subtle resentments and defenses than do children of other professions. Most often, rebellion and willful wrong do not show themselves in the life of a minister's child until many real or imagined injustices have heaped one upon the other. There have been children reared in Pentecostal parsonages who could not be reclaimed, once they flung themselves away from the church. The wounds and grudges that pained and burned through the years lay deeper than anyone realized.

Preaching gets hold of a person as no other work in life. Few professions so completely demand the whole person as does the ministry—the power of speech, the contagion of personality, the capacity to organize and administer, the capacity for insight, and the capacity to love, to feel, to help, to heal, to discipline, and to guide. Sometimes the minister is used so totally that he has little time or emotional energy left for his family. He has so many opportunities in his ministry to exercise his paternal impulses that it is possible for him to feel little urge to be a real parent in his home, but rather he desires for the family to be solicitous toward him.

The "don't-bother-me" kind of father should have stayed a bachelor. When he married, he knew that he would most likely be a father. No man has a right to be a father unless he means to be a good one. Somewhere in the midst of a church's busy program there must be a family program. This is imperative if the family is to be well balanced. There should be a place somewhere to talk about Bill's bicycle, Joe's algebra, and Mary's new dress. To have church for breakfast, dinner, and supper is like a doctor's family making a hospital of their home. There never need be any reason for embarrassment or self-condemnation because that, in the midst of a very busy schedule, a pastor will take some time to be with his family. Such action needs no explanation. In the midst of seventy years there are twenty and more that he must share with the children he chooses to bring into this world.

A six-year-old daughter of a politician was given a little dog, which she named Laddy. Soon she and the dog were faithful companions; one was constantly in the company of the other. Then one day, while the girl was at school, a truck ran over Laddy and killed him.

Mother was surprised that there were no tears when she told the girl—just a serious face, and then the girl ran out to play.

Soon the mother heard her calling, "Laddy, Laddy, come here." The mother called the girl in and again explained that the dog was dead. Suddenly the child burst into tears. "Mommy, oh Mommy," she cried, "I thought you said Daddy, not Laddy."

That story, of course, could send a chill through many a preacher's heart. For some it is too close to home for comfort. The child is not to blame. She did not care for her father because she was not taught to care. It might be that her father felt the same way about her. Let the following incident illustrate.

An educator said it became his duty to tell a preacher that his son was in serious difficulty. The preacher listened, still and silent. "I felt sure," the educator said, "that here was a father we could count on. When I had finished, his first remark was, 'I can never preach again.' For a moment I was stunned. Finally, I said, 'Sir, I am afraid if you ever help your son you will have to do it as a father.'"

Facts are stubborn things. It is a fact that it takes much home life to rear a family successfully. Certain things in a child's development are basic. The minister cannot bypass them without the deficiency having a far-reaching effect.

Home life and church work were not meant to conflict; on the contrary, each should complement the other. The better the father, the better the pastor; the better the guide for his own children, the better the guide for the children of others.

If a minister arises at 7:00 A.M. and goes promptly to work each day at 8:00, taking little or no time for lunch, he should have a good day's work done by 4:00 P.M. By 7:00 P.M. he has had time both to relax himself and also enjoy his family. On his day off, he can have more time with them. It is doubtful whether a frenzied approach God's work wrings out any more accomplishments in the long run than a steady, consistent, well-ordered workday. When we factor in the detriment of a lost child and his actions to a pastor's ministry, any gain seems nonexistent.

When the pastor and wife hurry the children to bed after church, so they might have their needed rest for school, and then take themselves to rest soon after, they will have from seven to eight hours of sleep. By consistently sleeping at night as they ought to and working hard in the day, they will have time to be with the children before the day closes. If the time does not seem available after he has systematically discharged the hours of a full day, the preacher is justified in taking it anyway, without feeling guilty. This time is not just for the minister personally, but for his wife and the children whom God gave them. People might criticize a minister for absenting himself from church work for a hunting or fishing trip, but no one can gainsay an arrangement that he makes simply for the sake of his family.

The time and fellowship that a minister has with his children is necessary because of the peculiar problems that the preacher's child faces. Most children of Pentecostal ministers are able to dress and live on the material level with the average child. There are, however, other things that could cause a complex. Problems that other children never face confront the child of the preacher. Since they have personal pride, ego, and desire for acceptance, just as any other child, they have major emotional adjustments to make. The stage of life in which young people yearn to be accepted by their peers is a dangerous one for children of ministers. To be rejected as a square and a sissy is a blow to youthful ego that hurts more than most adults even try to realize. If the young man or woman attempts to prove that he or she is not only a "regular guy" but a little more, then someone is about to be embarrassed in the parsonage or in the church.

It does not take much insight to understand why a minister's child would resent the glass house he lives in. No one wants to always be public property, having each action weighed on a set of scales different from what weighs the actions of others his own age.

There is no question that the higher the standard of holiness the pastor lifts, the more difficult will be the role of his children. The pastor's sermon and the preacher's children are somehow always being compared. The preacher who has little conviction and who had rather let a problem slide than judge it in righteous judgment, can allow his children more leeway with public criticism. This makes it very nice if the man-pleaser's conscience allows him not to think of the end result that his compromise has on the church and its families, and of the worldliness that will also touch his own. The little boys and girls whose preacher fathers take a stand against movies, mixed bathing, television, dancing, and the use of alcoholic beverages will find the grudge that the world has for their fathers falling, in part, upon their own shoulders.

When they bring these problems back to the parsonage, though they seem to mention them only casually at the supper table, the pastor-father should receive them with as much consideration as the most intricate problem that might confront him in church administration. It is here that he must not fail his own as a father. He should lovingly offer counsel that is both understandable and workable, along with the assurance that if they need him he will always be there. A martyr complex breeds resentment that might later fester into rebellion.

With care and prayer it is possible for the preacher to convince his children that they are fortunate to live in the parsonage. They meet many people, have many friends, and travel more widely than the average child. He can teach them neither to scorn other children nor to look up to them. They are equal in all things, and if their home life is healthy, the preacher's children may not only be at ease among others, but, in allowable fields, a leader. They can learn to disagree without being disagreeable and to refuse something without being offensive. The good pastor-parent can convince his children that Christ's way is the best way, the joyous way, and the happy way.

It is simply untrue that preacher's children are mostly bad. This conception is both erroneous and libelous. According to statistics, the average minister's son is above the ordinary. Anyone examining a copy of *Who's*

Who in America will find two preacher's children for every one of any other profession. While most of them are not Pentecostal, many of the same circumstances that prompted their success are common in the Pentecostal parsonage.

The minister should not make a showcase of the parsonage. Some plants grow better in the shade. The glare of public scrutiny directed toward the parsonage is keen enough without the pastor's using incidents of family life to illustrate his sermon. As much as possible, the pastor's family life should be dissociated from the eye of the church. Children need to grow up naturally, relaxed and secure.

When parents conscientiously deny something to children, they should casually replace it with something just as enjoyable but wholesome and allowable. They should prohibit nothing on the basis of a minister's office, but any restriction should rest on personal and individual righteousness. It is dangerous to continually bring the priesthood into the home. A pastor's children hear him as a preacher at church; they need the counsel of a father in the home.

Each child needs to be taught personally the love of Jesus and to pray. Prayer is best taught by demonstration. The most profound impressions concerning prayer have been upon children who often heard their parents praying. If a child has a solid personal relationship with God through love and prayer, and continues that relationship, most of a parent's worries are over.

The minister should never make a promise, especially to a child, unless there is no doubt that he can keep it. No child will trust a person unless he can believe his word;

and, above all else, a parent needs the confidence of his children.

The pastor should take care in instructing others how to rear their children. No one is perfect. When he gives advice, the pastor can always inject words that convey a humble attitude and an admission of his own limitations and failures.

None of the things we have mentioned are sufficient when considered alone, nor will any policy give the pastor the happy, well-ordered home that he wants and needs, unless he gives part of himself.

5

Getting Started in the Ministry

The young person who contemplates the ministry is often beset with many anxieties. Among the various misgivings peculiar to one who is soon to finish his prescribed course of study is that of employment. "Will the doors open to me? Will I be able to deliver the goods, or will my life be a flop? Am I under the control of life's eddies, or can I know the full flow of success?"

A biased opinion might be that finding an opportunity should pose no problem in the ministry. After all, thousands of towns have never heard the gospel. Millions upon millions have not had a personal confrontation with this message. Why should it be hard to get started in the ministry? These opinions have their merit, but the deduction is not conclusive. If it were that simple, the evangelization of America would be assured.

The minister's business is people—people who have

psychological quirks, mental blocks, and personal inhibitions. The preacher must do a sales job on these people. Their minds must be changed, their fears allayed, and their hearts made hungry. The most careless observer will note that the novice can anticipate disappointments, and everyone tries to avoid failure. It is true that the more extroverted can plow across the fertile fields without extra assurance and, in spite of floundering and glaring mistakes, accomplish something for God, but not everyone is like this.

Most people will not go at all unless another goes a little way with them. They realize that they cannot preach well. They need the experience of preaching, and of preaching to people who are kind enough to listen. This situation is found only in organized churches where pastors will allow them to "practice" upon patient people who are kindly interested in the young fledgling just trying out his wings. The ministerial apprentice cannot hope for this consideration on the raw home mission front, and he knows it. His anxious admission is often, "If I can just get started! A few revivals behind me would help me to get the feel of this thing. All I ask is a toehold, and then I feel I would be willing to go anywhere."

There are other areas besides preaching where the young minister does not feel sure of himself. He senses that his judgment is unqualified because of lack of experience, and he would like a chance to be watched over for a while as he comes to grips with the actual ministry. He needs a sounding board for his hesitant opinions. This is nothing to be ashamed of. The apostle Paul himself needed the extended hand of Barnabas before he found his respective field of labor. Why should we be surprised for a ministerial student to likewise encounter problems at this point?

Others need to acknowledge these reflections in the heart of the young preacher, and with approval. Such pondering indicates an appreciation of what lies before him. He has, at least in part, counted the cost. Cognizance of the problems at hand will precipitate in him a readiness to make the most of every opportunity that presents itself. In fact, the ministerial hopeful who does not approach his debut with eager anxiety might prove too uncaring to pay the full price of success.

The ministerial candidates should be so eager to get into the ministry that they are willing to crawl in order to carry out the great call of their lives. Young ministers who enter the evangelistic work, knowing that the pastor is doing them a favor by even allowing them in the pulpit, have tried to make up for their insufficiency by mowing the church lawn, sweeping the church, washing dishes, or even washing and waxing the pastor's car. This attitude does not hurt them but rather adds to their ministry. They are eager and hungry, and such people cannot be stopped.

A young preacher should not feel insulted when he is invited to preach in a youth service instead of on a Sunday night. He should count himself fortunate that he was not overlooked altogether. Each time, he needs to preach his very best, not for personal grandiosity but for the honest good that can be done. The smaller churches will be his field for a while, and maybe always. That area of God's vineyard needs the gospel, and he is fortunate to have a roof over his head. God will never let sincere faithfulness go unrewarded, and there are many benefits—

spiritual and otherwise—that come to those who work near the people. Many who have traveled the evangelistic road testify that the financial remuneration was often equal in smaller churches to what they received from the larger ones.

If a young single man contemplates the ministry, it is best for him to remain single until he gets two or three years of preaching experience behind him. The first few years are very precarious and often discouraging. Only a sure knowledge of God's call will cause him to swallow his pride, quiet his impatience, and convince him to wait and try again. More than one tired young wife of an evangelist who has traveled east and west to pick up a revival here and there has been heard to wearily remark, "I wonder if we will ever amount to anything. I wonder if we will ever be in demand as evangelists or have a church to pastor." Such a woman knows how disappointed her husband is when someone cancels a meeting at the last moment, or how hard it is to go for weeks without anyone asking him to preach. The added responsibility of a wife will not lighten the load, even if she is talented.

As we previously stated, the first meetings are often offered to the unskilled and unproven preacher solely as a gesture of goodwill. It is a sacrifice to a church and also to the pastor, especially if the evangelist stays in his home. But the inconvenience is not so great if he is a single man. The pastor's wife is not as concerned about the care of the house or the quality of the meal. For some reason, women are more at ease entertaining a male preacher than they are another woman. Strangely, they can harbor a psychological fear of one another. Thus an invitation to a single young man involves less sacrifice on the part of the pastor, and so it is easier to obtain than if he were married.

To enable him to travel widely and accept all possible invitations, irrespective of income, the young preacher needs as little financial obligation as possible. Here, again, the young single man's ministry is more flexible than that of the married man. He can practically live on fast food for a period of time in order to preach. Once he has equipped himself, it is so important that he preach as much as possible. After all, is not that precisely what he was called to do? Is there a true preacher who does not preach? Preaching is urgent, and the young man should absolutely keep himself clear of anything that would subtract from his preaching possibilities. The business at hand is preaching, and it must come first now and forever.

A single preacher must preach well enough to carry himself, but if he marries he must preach better. However, if his wife is dedicated, talented, and consecrated to the work, she can add to his ministry, especially if her talent is better than that offered by the local church where they might minister.

To a young minister, the foremost thing should not be marriage, but getting out into the ministry. He must preach, and that in abundance, if he aspires to a preaching ministry of any kind. If he is fortunate enough to be taken under the care of an interested pastor as an assistant, he will have the opportunity to develop the administrative side of his ministry first and pick up his preaching more gradually. But if he intends to break into the ministry by way of the evangelistic field, he must give himself wholly to its art and call. That is why, for the first few years, he needs to stay a free and unobligated young man, so that no financial urgency or inconvenience can rob him of one single chance to preach a sermon, fill an appointment, or attend a conference or camp meeting. He is, first of all, a minister of the gospel, obligated to God, called to the salvation of the lost, and he must preach whether he ever has a wife or any material substance or not.

Let us note the words of Lacordaire, a fervid minister of the Methodist Church in 1870: "Then go, fearing neither difficulties of foreign tongues, nor the differences of manners, nor the power of secular governments. Consult not the course of rivers, nor direction of mountain ranges: go straight on. Go as the thunder of Him who sent you—as the creative word went which carried life into chaos, as the eagles go, and the angels."

If the young preacher is already married or insists on being married, it is hoped that his wife is "parsonage material." It is not only important when he marries, but also whom he marries. So far as the minister is concerned, the choice of a wife is next in importance to the divine calling itself. If the young preacher ever honestly prayed about anything, he had better pray about a wife. Even with all sincerity, there is a chance in such a personal decision that he may not be sure just how absolute God's will is. He needs to use common sense. He should consider his prospective bride's home background, disposition, talent, personality, consecration, and love for God's work. There are lazy women, complaining women, gloomy women, bossy women, meddling women, and women too painfully proper; but there are others who seem to be born for preachers' wives. The preacher's wife must be dedicated wholly to God's work, if their life

78

together is to redound to a successful ministry.

Happy is the man who can paraphrase Dr. Leslie Weatherhead's statement thus: "My brother, God has given me a wife to whom I may turn, who ministers to me without weakening me, who accepts me when I am embittered with all the stress and strain of life, and by love's alchemy, has turned that bitter into sweet, saving my belief in humanity by her own. She hushes my fevered spirit. She laughs with me. She rejoices in my success without making me vain. She goes down with me into the deep places of failure without making me morbid. She receives me when I have made an utter fool of myself and without blinding her eyes and mine to my foolishness, she helps me to see life steadily and see it whole. She often listens to my hot, foolish, resentful words and waits with quiet eyes like homes of silent prayer, until the storm is past, and then, without letting me pose as a martyr on the one hand, and without argument on the other hand, she guides my feet into the way of peace. A tough job, but by claiming the grace and strength of the Lord, she is able to fill the bill."

It is very important that the woman who marries a preacher have a personal dedication to the work of God. The young preacher and his wife often grow up together into spiritual maturity, yet each must have the personal touch with Christ, communion and fellowship with Him alone, that makes for individual growth in the Lord. There are unfortunate instances where a young woman deceives herself and her young suitor by an apparent surrender to the work of Christ during courtship. After the marriage, the superficiality of her faith becomes evident. It is essential that the young preacher be sure that the girl of his dreams is a child of God with strong convictions concerning holiness, separated unto the Lord.

A minister's wife must be yielded to the call of God for His service as an individual with single-eyed devotion to her Lord. She must know how to pray, how to reach God so that His power is loosed. There will be many situations, unknown to her husband, when she must pray fervently and expectantly. She needs a sense of humor and a deep love for people, combined to enable her to endure disappointments, misunderstanding, foibles of people, and the irritations that constantly arise. To be able to see the funny side in the midst of stress is a lifesaver, for it dissipate the strain and helps one obtain a more objective point of view.

There is no doubt that the preacher's wife affects the preacher's getting started into the ministry. If an evangelist's wife is lazy about the pastor's home, not sharing in the work of the house, be the revival ever so good, the likelihood of their being recommended further will be lessened. If the pastor's wife does not appreciate certain things about the evangelist's wife, the knowledge of this sometimes goes before the young couple, detracting from their already limited opportunities.

The evangelist's wife can be the greatest asset. Many a ministry has been enhanced by the glory of a wife's unimpeachable Christian life. If the evangelist's wife is not able to contribute to the service with musical talent, she must work harder at other things that she can do, unless her husband's ministry is so strong and productive that he can carry them both. If he is just beginning, this would be doubtful, so both husband and wife need to be on their toes, doing all they can in these early days. After all, the plain fact is, he is not a guest, but in secular terms, simply hired to get a certain job done.

Child evangelism, Sunday school training, youth work, and many other things that add to the local church might be offered by the nonmusical evangelist's wife. The people who succeed anywhere are those who go beyond the expected. Such people shine in the ministry like new silver dollars, especially when it is all through the love of God and for His glory.

A young couple who complains about the treatment they received in other places is not going to be received with ease into the confidence of the host, for "the dog that will bring a bone, will carry one." No matter how sharply he is disappointed in a pastor, or how shabbily he feels he has been treated, the young minister should keep his feelings to himself. The host pastor and wife daily weigh him, not with malice but in curiosity. To live under the same roof for two or three weeks and not speak evil of another gives him credit. They are confident, then, that neither will he speak evil of them, so they lower their guard. They like him because they trust him, and thus they become friends who perhaps will speak well of him to a friend of theirs.

A young wife may be shy and not able to speak well from the platform. Some women have little or no ability to bless an audience in any way. If the young woman is dedicated and has a good Christian background, however, there is a fine chance that she will, in later years, make such a wonderful pastor's wife that all of her other deficiencies will be forgotten.

One of the finest things that can happen to a young man just coming out of Bible school, is to be invited to serve as an assistant under a gifted and successful pastor. Even if the salary is less than adequate, he should not pass by the opportunity. If the church is of such a size as to yield first-hand observation of broad administrative procedures, the offer is all the more advantageous. The young preacher's decision here should be based on the opportunity offered for further learning and experience. There are a few areas in life where thinking of self-interest is justified. One of these is treasuring the golden years of learning.

A young minister may be tempted to accept the offer of a friend to take a secular job and settle in his church as his assistant. Often this situation is not good if the goal is full-time ministry. Under such an arrangement he could easily find himself being no more than a job-holding, busy saint. However, if he has carefully and wisely evaluated his ministry to be something other than preaching, such a proposal might be a graceful way out of an awkward situation. Credit is to be given to the person, who, in discovering he was mistaken in his call, has the grace and courage to step down. Why would any honorable person care to perpetuate misconception? This decision cannot be a mere giving up under discouragement, for the real call of God is not disposed of that easily.

Among many aspiring preachers, regardless of age, there seems to be a tremendous urge to secure their license and to complete the various other steps that will bring them to full ordination. However, licensing, they soon discover, does not make the preacher. Unless a person has some hope of getting into the ministry, he should never announce his call. To do so and never initiate it is only to embarrass himself and create an awkward situation for others.

A man who held a high position in the United Pentecostal Church was heard several times to say, "I can't say that I ever heard God call me to preach. He simply asked me if I would work for Him, and I said that I would." More than one honest person has said, "I feel that I am called of God to work in some capacity, but not to preach." The struggling person who is making no apparent headway at getting into the active ministry will find that hurrying to get his license does not help the situation but, in the long run, further complicates it. In the final analysis, it is a person's ministry itself that recommends him, rather than his credentials. License and ordination come in due course as the ministry is developed and the preacher begins to put "corn in the crib."

The family man who feels called of God but whose years and finances prohibit his going to Bible college, or who cannot get out on the field, must do all he can locally. The pitfall for such a man is that he may become stalemated. He may live only in vague hope that something will turn up, and all the while his attention is diverted from his call by the same problems and pressures with which any other workingman must contend. Consequently, he sits uncomfortably in a position where he is unhappy and where others tend to misunderstand and even resent.

In time, this quandary kills whatever initiative the hopeful family man ever had and causes him to lose confidence in himself. Perhaps this is the reason why in certain localities there can be many inactive local preachers. In the same locality there may be six hospitals, four jails, and six rest homes for the aged. In addition, in the same area there might be a skid row with vacant store buildings.

Abundance of ministerial work goes undone every day in such situations all over the nation. If much-needed services are ever administered in these places, it is often by the hand of a pastor who already has more than he can possibly handle.

In one town, jail services were never held until a young man just filled with the Holy Ghost took it upon himself, as a layperson, to do what he could. Meanwhile, local-licensed preachers were in the area hoping for a place to get started, while it waited at their doorstep. Despise not the day of small things. (See Zechariah 4:10.)

The called family man should wholeheartedly apply himself in these waiting fields because they offer an incentive for further effort. A person will ordinarily not prepare a sermon unless he has hopes of preaching it. Even the anticipation of preaching it in the jail offers some impetus for study. A ministry employed is a ministry that grows. After all, visiting the sick and shut-ins is the same thing he would be doing were he pastoring a church. It is a puzzle and a shame that some local preachers are the least dependable soulwinners and workers in a local church. If a person will give himself unstintingly to ministerial work, helping the pastor and pushing the local church program extensively, his gift will grow and, in time, will of itself make way for him.

Most young preachers know better than to take an old, well-established church at the opening of their ministry, even if it were offered to them. Latent troubles and grievances often lie unsettled in churches of some age. Such an arrangement could become his graveyard, or leave him so badly mauled that he would be years recovering. On the other hand, if a church is very run down, with only a few attending, it may be an open door to service for a beginner. Especially does this arrangement lend itself to the older man with a family and a job who is trying to break into the ministry. More than one United Pentecostal Church and preacher are doing well today who found one another under similar circumstances. Both the church and the preacher needed and wanted a chance, hence the result had to be good.

Generally speaking, however, when the church is self-supporting, having had several pastors and its share of church trouble, the novice should discreetly steer clear. There might be a reason why he was asked to come. Some church boards are willing to bear with inexperience for the pleasure of running the preacher, along with the church. It is better to attempt a new work under the watchful eye of a friend than to have an established work fold up under an inexperienced hand.

6

The Minister and His Preaching

The Christian ministry derives authority from Jesus Christ, the originator, and not from Moses or the prophets or even from John the Baptist. It was a new device for the propagation of the faith that He came to establish in the earth. The principal business of the ancient priests was to offer sacrifices and that of the prophets to foretell the future events, but that of Christian ministers is to preach the gospel—"the good news"—in such a manner as to command the acceptance of its benefits.

The commission under which they act reads, "Go ye into all the world, and preach the gospel to every creature. He that believeth and is baptized shall be saved; but he that believeth not shall be damned" (Mark 16:15-16). Judaism was chiefly limited to a single nation. Christianity extends its sympathies and provisions alike to all nations and to every individual. It makes religion a personal business and the salvation of souls the grand object of its ministers. They are to preach with special reference to this result—not human science or opinions, but the gospel—not to glorify themselves or entertain the people, but to help people see their lost condition, repent of their sins, and be filled with the Holy Ghost.

Paul, who was called to be an apostle, understood the matter in this light. Speaking of Christ, he said: "Whom we preach, warning every man, and teaching every man in all wisdom; that we may present every man perfect in Christ Jesus: whereunto I also labour, striving according to his working, which worketh in me mightily" (Colossians 1:28-29). And again, "Now then we are ambassadors for Christ, as though God did beseech you by us: we pray you in Christ's stead, be ye reconciled to God" (II Corinthians 5:20).

Acting on this understanding of their commission, the apostles "went forth, and preached every where, the Lord working with them, and confirming the word with signs following" (Mark 16:20). Those who now preach the true gospel for this purpose, who really desire and intend to save sinners, do much the same thing and with the same results.

Failure in fruitfulness often comes from diversion. It is possible to lose sight of the proper object of preaching and seek to defend the gospel, or discourse intelligently about it for general effect, rather than preach it for individual faith and immediate conversion. We must not forget that the gospel's best vindication and its highest charms are in its saving results. Casting out one demon by the power of God and seeing one lowly sinner filled with the Holy Ghost will go further in defending the gospel than many well-planned arguments. Since the gospel is the power of God unto salvation, when we present it properly, it will demonstrate itself and carry conviction to hearts that no intellectual reasoning can effect. The minister stands in Christ's stead to seek the lost and lead them to heaven. The man of God should feel that his main task is to save souls. It is not his business to preach a certain number of sermons or to take care of this or that meeting, but to save as many as possible, to bring as many sinners as he can to repentance, and with all available power attempt to build them up into holiness. The more directly a minister comes to grips with this work, the better he will be understood, and the more likely he is to succeed.

Salvation—necessary, immediate, and possible now—to the perishing sinner must be the theme in which all of preaching, prayers, and tears center, and to which they all tend. It was for this that Christ died, and for this the Holy Ghost strives and all of heaven awaits. If someone is a true minister, his thoughts, studies, and labors will be shaped with reference to this grand object. He may err in his judgment and methods, but his intention will be to lead people to Christ, and in this he will not fail.

In chapter one we stated that a requisite of great preaching is a definite and positive call, laid warm and unmistakable upon the heart of the minister, to preach. It is noticeable in tracing the history of great preachers that the most successful of them were characterized by a thorough conviction of sin. The Wesleys were terribly awakened, and crucified themselves with many fastings, prayers, and self-denials, crying out of the depths when God put a new song into their mouths. Whitefield was so distressed when in prayer for mercy that the sweat dropped from his face. "God only knows," he wrote, "how many nights I have lain upon my bed groaning under what I felt. Whole days and weeks have I spent in lying prostrate on the ground in silent or vocal prayer." Though these men may not have been baptized with the Holy Ghost, who doubts that this terrible conviction of sin played its part in their success as ministers in their day?

Powerful, soul-shaking convictions are indispensable to the ministry. The sure conviction of Saul of Tarsus laid the foundation of his wonderful conversion and usefulness. No subsequent education can atone for the absence of this experience. Denominations begin at once to deteriorate when preachers come to their pulpits knowing nothing of soul-shattering experience with God involving the shame of their sin and the joy of its forgiveness.

Webster's definition of preaching is "to proclaim or cry aloud." This is something that Pentecostal preachers are well known for. When one suddenly enters into the presence of a fervent preacher who is building toward the climax of a powerful sermon, he might be prone to question, as did one woman, "Why the loud voice? Why do you get so excited?" This woman had driven up to an open-air tabernacle midway in the sermon and found the man of God captivated by the unction of his thought. The loudness of the speaker's voice, the pathos, the voice tone, and emotional fervency seemed uncalled for to her.

Perhaps only the men of God who preach to save can understand what really happens to a preacher when he is anointed to preach. But to be successful one must come before the people full of divine feeling and speaking from a sincere heart. If the person is called, if he is humble, true and holy, there will generally come to him a mysterious unction that gives power to his thoughts, words, voice, and gestures. Art cannot produce it; chains cannot bind it; mountains cannot bury it. It thaws the most icy habits. It bursts from the lips. It speaks from the eye. It modulates the tone. It pervades the manner. It possesses and controls the whole person. The preacher is visibly in earnest, he convinces, he persuades. He preaches, while the mere orator performs. One presents God and truth as he feels them; the other, as he has learned them. The utterances of the first are the breathings of a living, throbbing soul; those of the last, the studied expressions of art.

Bible-Centered Preaching

It is evident that neither Jesus nor His disciples sermonized as many are prone to do today. They simply gave discourses on a truth in question or one they felt the congregation needed. Most of their utterances were initiated by a current issue for which the people needed an answer. In such situations, the common interest was already aroused on the subject and the congregation was waiting for the dissemination of information.

Both Christ and the apostles sometimes raised an issue and launched themselves forthrightly into the discussion of it. For instance, Jesus raised the question, "Which is the greatest, the altar or the gift on the altar?" And Paul frankly told the Athenians that they were too superstitious and began at once to disclose to them the identity of the "Unknown God." Where there is no apparent outstanding issue at hand that would be profitable to use, one must be raised and that usually by way of a text.

The text allows a minister to incite the interest of his hearers in a more specific way than an ordinary lecture might do. The text furnishes the preacher a solid basis of instruction on a subject that he feels the congregation should consider. Using scriptural texts gives variety to preaching and aids the memory of the hearers.

A preacher must not select his text solely upon the hope of having something original and nice, rather than appropriate and powerful. The text should mean something in itself and naturally introduce the subject on which the preacher will be speaking. Texts that in themselves require a long explanation are a burden rather than a help. Odd texts are seldom effective texts, as they tend to magnify either the frivolity or the cleverness of the preacher, and in the process a firm truth is lost.

Each time a minister preaches, he should strive to explain the subject at hand as much as time allows, using enough illustrations to make his message interesting as well as instructive. He should select texts that embrace fundamental truth, such as repentance, faith, redemption, regeneration, sanctification, holiness, the resurrection, judgment, heaven, hell, and so on. Great subjects that move the feelings, questions that have agitated the world and stirred hearts, problems that people would like to settle before they die, and subjects about which they would ask Jesus or an apostle if it were possible, are always powerful sermon topics.

The preacher should not tone down or explain away the biblical texts but urge their acceptance. They can be mighty arguments for immediate repentance and holiness if presented in a way that the hearers can see that the minister believes them in his heart and expects his hearers to be lost unless they espouse them also. These are things that change people. Sound, solid, truthful preaching is the only road to success for a Pentecostal minister.

The preacher should hold the Scriptures in awe, remembering the words of Revelation 22:19, which declares that if anyone takes anything away from what is written in the book, his part will be taken out of the holy city and out of the blessings of the Book. And if he adds anything to it, the plagues that are written in the Book will be added to him.

There is no end of the variety of worthless subjects that have been forced into the pulpit to supplant the real, saving gospel. Even when ministers succeed in displaying considerable ability on these lines, they never fail to show their own spiritual emptiness. God save Pentecostal preachers from such folly! Let each sermon be preached so that if it shall prove to be the last sermon the people shall ever hear, it will be sufficient to lead them to the Lord, or draw them closer to Him.

One preacher asked another minister why he now used so much more Scripture than formerly. He recalled how he had seen him read his text, close his Bible, and lay it aside for the rest of the sermon; but now it was not so, and he wondered why. The thoughtful reply of the questioned brother was, "I have found that the Word of God is much more effective than anything that I could say myself." And it is. It is the authority and the power of God unto salvation.

Since this is so, preaching should always be Bible-centered. We see the merit of such preaching in the one Bible-centered sermon that Philip preached to the lone sinner in the desert. Philip's preaching was from Isaiah 53, and from that chapter he preached Christ. Somehow, when he preached Christ he also preached water baptism in His name, and that is just as it should be. The record shows that this Bible-centered approach was effective.

One good Pentecostal minister, after having met someone who had a very interesting story of his life to tell, though the final end was disappointment, made a decision. "From here on," he stated, "all I care for is the story of Jesus. Just tell me the story of Jesus, and that will be sufficient." Perhaps he was right, in that the story of Jesus can never be supplanted. The message of the Cross must always be supreme, for Jesus said, "And I, if I be lifted up from the earth, will draw all men unto me" (John 13:32). Paul knew this and said, "I determined not to know any thing among you, save Jesus Christ, and him crucified" (I Corinthians 2:2).

Always at His Best

Preachers are "ambassadors for Christ," called to persuade people to be "reconciled to God" (II Corinthians 5:20). Paul said:

"For though I be free from all men, yet have I made myself servant unto all, that I might gain the more. And unto the Jews I became as a Jew, that I might gain the Jews; to them that are under the law, as under the law, that I might gain them that are under the law; to them that are without law, as without law, . . . that I might gain them that are without law. To the weak became I as weak, that I might gain the weak: I am made all things to all men, that I might by all means save some" (I Corinthians 9:19-22).

It is true that a preacher must do many things and be many things to many people while he is fulfilling the tenure of his service to the Lord, but woe to the one who loses sight of preaching as his first great responsibility. He has to be an administrator, a counselor, and a go-between, but his main business is preaching, and to that end he was called.

Where Pentecostal churches are unable to support themselves, and the pastor must work, it can usually be expected that the preaching will be less than it should be. This is not to the discredit of any good man who has the courage to extend his ministry into such adverse circumstances. The very fact that he is willing to carry the double load is a credit to him, but the fact stands that preaching, in order to be great, must be the main business of the preacher.

Often, after a week of toil, the working preacher feels the need of relaxation on Saturday evening. He may spend time with friends or relatives, until the minister at length observes that he must go study for the next day. But upon arriving home and looking over his Sunday school lesson, he finds himself more sleepy than he thought. So he promises himself to rise early and study more, but quite often he sleeps longer than intended. The morning of hurry about the house, not at all conducive to spiritual study, finds him having to thumb through his Bible on the way to church, hoping to find something that he can impart to the people. Preaching like this usually begets weak churches that are inattentive, bored, worldly, and sickly. This is not because the pastor wants it that way. Perhaps the day will come when ministers can be a greater help one to another and lighten the load of those who would like to employ themselves altogether in God's good work.

If they are not careful, preachers who are well supported can also allow themselves to be sidetracked from the fulfillment of their holy calling. For instance, it is fatal to get involved in politics. The fortunes of a given party ebb and flow, and a church that has given its allegiance to one side or the other will find itself on the elevator of public opinion, its popularity either going up or down. The influence of the church should not be attached to things so unstable. History shows that when the church has played with politics, she has done so to her own hurt.

Our forefathers' interest in this world was strictly limited. They counted themselves strangers and pilgrims upon this earth, seeking a city to come. It is always better to deal in eternal verities and not in temporal power structures. Before Pilate, Jesus simply stated, "My kingdom is not of this world: if my kingdom were of this world, then would my servants fight" (John 18:36). While the minister should be a good citizen and seek to improve his community, there is not a preacher who can fix the social structure of society. His primary duty lies in preaching the gospel.

A preacher should avoid the role of a secular crusader. On moral issues, his sentiment and vote should be for a safer and more respectable community, but the wise minister knows that conditions do not change until people change, and the only thing that will affect that is the old-fashioned gospel.

In the days of the apostles, a condition existed that they could have crusaded against had they chosen. That condition was slavery. No one doubts that a human made in the image of God should not be sold as an animal and that to demand a person to work without financial remuneration is wrong. To deny a person his freedom and the right to choose and to lay up for his posterity is to defraud him of the rights of life. However, the New Testament church was born into a world of many slaves. It was not uncommon in the great Phrygian Valley, where the strong churches of Asia Minor were located, for one man to have as many as 1,200 slaves. But, strange as it may seem, not one passage in the New Testament directly condemns slavery. Several passages instruct servants (slaves) to have a Christian attitude toward their masters, and the masters toward the servants, but none explicitly says that slavery is wrong and that slave owners should cease from the practice. Yet history discloses that wherever the gospel has been preached and Christianity established, slavery has disappeared. God's method of changing situations is to change people. His appeal is to the heart, and that by the gospel. When people are changed, other things take care of themselves. The greatest contribution the preacher can make to society is to preach the gospel that saves from sin.

If a man of God believes this, it will stimulate him to study and pray that he may improve his preaching. It will be his delight to imitate the Master, who taught the people from the Scriptures at such times and places and by such methods as were best adapted to command their confidence and reform their lives. In this state of mind, begotten by the Holy Ghost, ministers will naturally speak as the Spirit gives them utterance, as did the apostles on the Day of Pentecost. When forbidden by the civil authorities they did not refrain, but continued speaking in the Temple, courts, prisons, and any other place where they could find opportunity. They seemed to have no set sermons, but they simply preached as the circumstances of the hour and their objects required. They were constrained to speak of what God had done and was doing for them, and what He was ready to do for others. They had little human preparation and only thought of preaching as they were moved by the Spirit. We must never lose this spiritual element if Pentecost is to remain as it should be.

It is very important that young ministers sufficiently appreciate and cultivate the proper spirit of their calling. The call and its anointing is everything, and no morality or intelligence or eloquence can take its place. Young ministers need above all things to be fully absorbed in their work, to burn with an intense desire to honor God and save souls from hell. They should feel all that is expressed in the following lines by an unknown author:

> I would the precious time redeem
> And longer live for this alone:
> To spend and to be spent for them
> Who have not yet my Savior known;
> Fully on these my mission prove
> And only breathe to breathe Thy love.
> My talents, gifts and graces, Lord,
> Into Thy blessed hands receive;
> And let me live to preach Thy Word;
> And let me for Thy glory live,
> My every sacred moment spend
> In publishing the sinner's Friend.

With this spirit there would be little wasting of time, little reading of fictitious material that diverts the mind from God and duty, little wasting of time in pointless conversations and all-night gabfests. Perhaps it would produce an instant and thorough revolution in the habits, studies, deportment, and preaching of many ministers who now imagine they are doing very well.

Surely no one can reach the highest degrees in any calling or profession unless he admires it, loves it, gives himself wholly to it, and has his mind full of it day after day. No painter ever became great who had art only as a collateral pursuit, or who did not reckon it the greatest of goals, or who did not sacrifice everything else for it. The preacher who concentrates his chief thoughts on something other than the ministry will be a drone, if not a Demas.

Importance of Preaching

It is not uncommon for someone to describe a service in which there was an unusual manifestation of the Spirit by saying, "We had a good service last night; we didn't have any preaching." This statement is not meant to reflect any disdain upon the ministry of the Word; it is just an attempt to reveal the degree of spiritual spontaneity present in the service. Woe be the day when God does not break in upon a service in times of glorious divine order, insomuch that it is either impossible or improper to launch into a sermon at that time. But just as emphatically we should state that so long as the church is in the world, the need of the preached Word of God will never be superseded. Pentecostal churches should be sound, solid, and based upon the teaching of God's Word. No church program, no showing of films or slides, no series of social functions can take the place of the preached Word.

The apostles pointed out this truth when they said, "It is not reason that we should leave the word of God, and serve tables. Wherefore, brethren, look ye out among you seven men of honest report, full of the Holy Ghost and wisdom, whom we may appoint over this business. But we will give ourselves continually to prayer, and to the ministry of the word" (Acts 6:2-4). They believed that the ministry of the Word was the most important thing.

Preaching, hot-hearted and true, begets revival. It is now, and always has been, the heart and core of all great revivals. Dwight Moody, Charles Finney, Jonathan Edwards, and Billy Sunday, all giants in preaching ability, demonstrate this fact. These men went to the pulpit for the express purpose of preaching their hearts out. They rose with tears in their eyes, thunder in their souls, and fire in their bones. To them hell was hot, heaven beautiful, sin black, and God pure.

Someone asked Billy Sunday why he was so successful in winning souls. Not answering immediately, he looked out of the window to a busy street below, and when he looked back, tears were on his cheek. Pointing to the streets filled with people, he simply said, "They are going to hell, they are going to hell, they are going to hell!" He felt that deep within his heart. That kind of feeling, that kind of warmth in a preacher's preaching always gets results.

As Jonathan Edwards preached his famous sermon, "Sinners in the Hand of an Angry God," people fell in the aisle, clung to the back of their pews, begged, screamed, and asked God not to let them go to hell. They could hardly wait until he had finished so they could rush down the aisle and fall at an altar of repentance. Strong, Bible-centered, anointed preaching begets revival.

When preaching declines, churches backslide. They always have and they always will. When sermons degenerate into lectures, when more is said about current events, the cosmos, and social obligations to the community than about the blood of Christ, the delivering power of God, the heat of hell and the beauty of heaven, spiritual decay is inescapable. When the strong flavor of the Word and Spirit is gone, when the minister does not state positively his text, join a lot more of God's Word with it, and declare clearly the things God said to do and not to do, spiritual declension and bored disinterest are sure to follow.

In a denomination where the minister becomes a psychologist and a lecturer instead of a preacher, the church ceases to be the voice of God and the minister becomes a priest instead of a prophet. Such churches then begin to manipulate rituals in the church service, hoping to leave behind a sanctimonious atmosphere. All the people receive is the sob of the organ and the beautiful order of a ritual, long, dead, and musty. The church went into the Dark Ages when preachers quit preaching and allowed ritual to take the place of the pulpit.

Sometime ago one of our presidents stated that we needed an Isaiah and a Paul. It is only the prophet's voice crying in the wilderness of our time that can turn people from their sinful ways. Until Jesus comes, there never will be a time when preaching will be superseded by something of greater importance.

Even the Sunday school, as important as it is, must be evangelized once a year or more. It is one thing to invite people to come to a discussion of God's Word and quite another to have a minister boldly stand before them and press the claims of Calvary upon their hearts. Students in each department should be called upon to give their hearts to God. There must come a definite, positive effort to bring children to an altar of repentance. As the churches grow, pastors should beware lest they become so involved in administrative matters that they are nothing more than executive officers instead of preachers of righteousness. It is a sad day for God's man when, instead of a study, he has an office from which he disseminates only plans and procedures and into which there flows only reports of various church functions.

Gene Edwards stated in his book *How to Have a Soulwinning Church* that a church ought to keep its program simple and that there is no need for a great cluster of committees. The best law is less law; the best government is less government. "This one thing I do," stated the apostle Paul. (See Philippians 3:13.) The call of the preacher is simply to preach the gospel.

A man on the radio once gave this invitation to his church: "Come visit us this weekend. Be with us this Sunday night. We are going to have a lot of singing and a little bit of preaching." But a musical program can never take the place of preaching. Nothing is to overshadow the Word of God. It is our guide, our meat, and our staff.

This is not to say that the Pentecostal minister must preach every night. Perhaps for several nights, on rare occasions, the Spirit may so move that there is no place for the ministering of the Word. Many preachers can testify that, after laboring long in sermon preparation, the Spirit notified them as soon as they came to the platform that there would be no preaching that night. But this is the exception and not the rule. The wise pastor knows that demonstrative worship alone will not suffice, that somehow he must anchor, root, and ground his congregation in the Word of the Lord if it is to stand.

There are three reasons why preaching is so effective. First, preaching instructs. It appeals to reason and intellect. It expounds, explains, and reveals. It makes God's Word more plain. Second, preaching melts the human heart. The emotion of the preacher, the fervor of the spirit that passes through him, goes with the Word of God when it is preached and falls heavy on the heart of the listener. Third, preaching calls upon the people for action. Most of the people today who are filled with the Holy Ghost in Pentecostal churches came in under the impetus of a powerful sermon, carried forth and laid hard by the Spirit against the door of their hearts.

What Should the Preacher Preach?

Perhaps we can best answer this question by another question. There is not a better starting point for the construction of a sermon than for the minister to ask himself, "What is the need of the specific situation?" Determining the need of the congregation at that particular time, and praying alone to God about it, will not only give him direction in his study but will prepare his heart for both the conception and the delivery of the sermon. No one should attempt to preach without aiming at some definite and immediate result.

Once in a while a sermon fails to indicate any purpose to convert people to God or to build them up in holiness. It relates more to matters of curiosity, without effecting an important point of faith or godliness. What was the purpose? If no one is instructed in righteousness and moved toward God, why should the sermon be preached at all? Could it be that the speaker had no care at all for the spiritual need present and thus did not attempt to rectify it with the fervent application of God's Word? Could it be that he rather endeavored to appear learned and clever, and thus present himself instead of Christ? This is trifling with God, with people, with time, and with eternity. It is an indirect way of saying that the tremendous doctrines of the Bible and the purpose of a called ministry are not as important as they appear to be.

Certain situations may require a fresh approach to catch people "with guile," as Paul claimed to do. But whatever the subject or text, the appeal must ever and always be to solid spiritual betterment, and a challenge must be extended at the close to act upon it.

A minister who is properly impressed with his responsibility will search his heart and ask himself, "What do I hope to effect here tonight with this congregation? What is the particular object that I want to achieve?" It may be one thing or another, but in his judgment it in some way either leads to the salvation of some soul or the encouragement of a saint to a more righteous life. This being settled, he will ask next, "What particular truth or subject is best, under the circumstances, to effect that object?" This question may be easily answered, or it may require much thought and prayer, and then perhaps left in doubt for some time. Usually the particular aspect of the subject to be presented at a given time depends on the circumstances.

The grand issue at the first was, "Is Jesus the promised Messiah?" The Jews denied it and pronounced Him an imposter. This rendered it necessary for the apostles to furnish the evidence to sustain His claims, hence their frequent reference to the prophecies concerning Him, His birth, character, miracles, and so on. Peter's argument on the Day of Pentecost was a strong specimen of apostolic preaching and was so mightily convincing that many cried out, "Men and brethren, what shall we do?" (See Acts 2:14-37.)

Later, Paul found it needful to preach against salvation by works, as taught by the scribes and Pharisees, and show it to be of grace. At other times, in conflict with Sadducees, he passed these points to prove the resurrection of the dead.

There are times when a preacher is called to minister to a congregation with which he is unacquainted and has no way of knowing a personal or collective need. Under such circumstances, it is best to present fundamental truth as related to life, which cannot be accepted without benefit or rejected without loss. The man of God should have such a personal conviction and appreciation of truth that he can simply preach truth for truth's sake, with fervency and sincerity, though he knows not its particular application to the present congregation. When the subjects have to do with such solid themes as service, holiness, spiritual thirst, repentance, and prayer, it is certain that the sermon will not altogether fall by the wayside.

People usually care little, and it is likely that God cares less, about theories or opinions that have no influence on the heart and life—speculative thoughts that reform no sinner and comfort no saint. Most people are practical and are inclined toward subjects that they can understand and put to good use in their own lives.

Preaching about nothing, or of ancient or absent sinners, is not likely to arouse a congregation to profitable living. People go to church to hear of themselves, their conditions, duty and destiny, and will not respect a preacher for long who has not the courage to speak out. They do not come to have their brains taxed but to have their hearts made warmer and their lives holier. If a minister can convince his congregation during the first five minutes that he cares for nothing but to get them to heaven, his critics will be very few, even though he does speak out forcefully.

The good pastor always has heavy upon his heart the needs of his people and always, through God, reaches out to meet and supply those needs in daily ministrations, in studies, and in sermons. He knows that some sit in his congregation who need relief from fear. He has looked often into the anxious face of fear and knows its corrosive blight. He is acquainted with the many and varied fears that sweep the souls of some of his parishioners. He has noted that even the prayers of some of his people did not rest upon faith but were born of desperation. He has seen them twist themselves into an emotional tangle that was void of all confidence in their effort to contact God. He knows that some of them simply played upon their nerves until what they took as a blessing from God was nothing more than an emotional reaction, and they were burning themselves out on the inside. The good pastor must reach out in compassion and attempt to teach them to love Jesus and trust Him as the dearest Father. He must try to show in his teaching and preaching that nothing can separate the honest, trying soul from the love of God.

The good pastor knows that his people need comfort. He knows directly or indirectly the smiting blows that lay his people low. He cares, and he knows that God cares. This attitude is reflected in sermons of comfort that flow out with much love and assurance to heal the broken-hearted.

The pastor is well acquainted with those who need to be led away from self into a larger and more fruitful life. Greek literature told of Narcissus, the mythical son of a river god. It was prophesied that the extremely handsome Narcissus would have a long life and be very beneficial, providing he never saw himself. But one day as he bent down beside the river to get a drink he saw handsome features in the water and after that he was never satisfied. He could get nothing worthwhile done, for he was always coming back to the river to look at himself. His life had lost its effectiveness.

Psychologists have coined the word *narcissism*, which means that a person is no longer able to look at life objectively but is caught up in the small world of self. Every decision is relative to his feelings and in accordance with what he is going to profit by it. The preacher knows that, in some way, he must attract the attention of these people away from self to the One who is greater than all. Many sermons are directed toward that object.

How good and true is the approach of a well-known Pentecostal preacher. When asked how he went about preparing his sermon and determining what he was going to preach on a given night, his answer was simple and altogether right. "Well," he said, "all I know to do is just get down on my knees and start praying. If I'm going to preach that night to sinners, I start praying for sinners and talking to the Lord about them. I pray for the sinners I know for sure will be there and for those I hope will

107

come. If I'm going to preach to the saints, I get down on my knees and start praying for saints, calling their names, and of course when I call their names their needs come up before me." And there it is. First, the preacher should go to prayer, praying about the needs of the congregation, and then to the Bible.

If a good pastor sees some of his young people drifting from the paths of righteousness, of course his heart is troubled, and he makes them the object of interceding prayer, calling their names and needs to God. Some of those whom he lifts up in his prayer may have a problem finding themselves, and in the process are stepping on many people's feelings and rights. With these strong feelings in his soul, it is not unusual that perhaps, as the pastor reads in his Bible the story of how a bully with the biggest iron chariot in town rode out in his rough way once too often, he shares the feelings of this man's mother when he did not return. In pain she cried through the lattice, "Why is his chariot so long in coming? Why tarry the wheels of his chariots?" She cried for a boy who never returned. (See Judges 5:28.)

Of course, the same principle works with any other of the various needs of a congregation. Most often the preacher feels the need impressed upon him by actual knowledge, or by God in the form of a strong mysterious burden. He goes to God, where his heart is warmed and prepared, and then to the Bible for proof and remedy.

Rapport

Rapport means the establishment of sympathetic understanding. Speech instructors stress the need of rapport between speaker and audience, stating that if the speaker does not secure it in the first part of his address, his effort will largely be lost. This is not altogether true in the field of preaching, since the minister does not always preach to please his congregation. He must first preach because it is right and because that particular truth is needed. This is done, of course, in the spirit of love. Such preaching in apostolic days sometimes ended in great revivals, and at other times resulted in the bloody murder of the preacher. Such fearless preaching produced a revival or a revolution, but it was not ignored. The end result was always the furtherance of the kingdom.

Revolutions that do not further the church of God, but leave people wounded, confused and bitter, evidently are not started by the same spirit that rocked cities in the days of the apostles. Within the church, "God is not the author of confusion, but of peace" (I Corinthians 14:33).

While the anointed Pentecostal preacher does not use the psychology of a politician in the pulpit, feeling that he must warm the people toward himself with a few jokes before he begins, he does gauge the depth, tone, and attitude of the service in a way that only God supplies before he comes to the pulpit. The mature, spiritual minister lets the song service speak to him and the testimonies tell him things. All the while, the Spirit leaves its keen impressions about the service upon his soul, telling him to change his message or assuring him that he is on the right track in his thought for the evening.

Before he ever comes to the pulpit, the Spirit-filled preacher has sensed the spiritual status of the congregation. He has sampled it, judged it, and located the people. Within himself he knows where the people are, and he knows where the Lord wants him to lead them. Such a person who has prayed much, studied well, and been assured by the Spirit during the preliminaries, comes to the pulpit with a bold assurance. He leaves the impression on the congregation that he has walked with God and knows what he is talking about. He comes in such a way that they feel he is under orders. The impression of Habakkuk 2:20 is left with them: "But the LORD is in his holy temple: let all the earth keep silence before him." This is the kind of rapport that Pentecostal preachers seek, which only the anointing of God can supply.

Perhaps the greatest wish any preacher could make relative to his ministry is for the two things that God gave to Jacob. After Jacob's all-night prayer and wrestling, God's promise to him was, "For as a prince hast thou power with God and with men" (Genesis 32:28). In the light of this, the compliment that a young preacher passed to another was indeed flattering: "You have a secret I would like to learn. You seem to sense the need of the congregation. When you approach them you have a way of bringing man and God together." This is precisely what the Pentecostal preacher strives for.

One great person has said, "One reason why we were never reluctant to obey our parents in the home was because our parents lived and conducted themselves in such a way that they left the impression upon us children that they also were under orders; that there was Someone higher than they whom they feared, as we feared them, and that obedience was simply the way of a normal life." It is this impression that the preacher should strive to leave as he comes to preach the Word that God has given him.

7

The Minister and Divine Leadership

Since the ministry is actually divine leadership, proper execution is an absolute necessity. The bold, assertive proclamation of truth will not be effective unless the preacher knows in his heart that he is in the will of God. The knowledge of being under the jurisdiction of a higher power imparts an assurance that earthly ability cannot equal.

A soldier one day based his faith in his request to Jesus upon the theory of absolute authority:

"The centurion answered and said, Lord, I am not worthy that thou shouldest come under my roof: but speak the word only, and my servant shall be healed. For I am a man under authority, having soldiers under me: and I say to this man, Go, and he goeth; and to another, Come, and he cometh; and to my servant, Do this, and he doeth it. When Jesus heard it, he marvelled, and said to them that followed, Verily I say

unto you, I have not found so great faith, no, not in Israel" (Matthew 8:8-10).

The centurion knew the value of being under authority and the influence such a position carried. He felt sure that the Master who ruled the wind and the waves had only to speak the word and the need would be taken care of. Jesus had never told him of His power, but the assurance and noble bearing of the Lord conveyed this impression to the centurion.

This sense of authority comes to the minister, and its impression extends to the audience when there is within his heart the feeling of divine right. There are times when the minister feels strongly this authoritative leadership, and there are other times that it is not so pronounced. Why is this? When one is sure that he is right in principle, right in spirit, and right in the center of God's will, this forceful attitude is a part of his life. This does not mean that he should throw his weight around and become overbearing in his behavior. However, there is a strong sense of assurance and direction that is entirely within the bounds of all other Christian precepts. When a minister is not sure of God's will, or is not strongly convinced of the position he is assuming, the trumpet gives an uncertain sound. For the sake of positiveness and assurance, the preacher needs divine leadership.

Divine leadership is able to promote the kingdom of God as nothing else can. Paul did not arrive in Ephesus two years late, as carnal reasoning might have had him to believe, but he arrived right on time. Philip was on the road south just in time to intercept the eunuch's chariot. Tremendous growth came about on the mission fields because the Holy Ghost directed that the church should lay no greater burden upon the Christian Gentiles than was necessary.

Divine leadership does not always lead to pleasant paths, but it always promotes the kingdom of God. This is one of the true tests of any enterprise or decision. In the long run, did it actually promote the kingdom of God?

Divine leadership elevates the office of the ministry. It may not always elevate a particular minister, but in the long run it wins a respect for preachers who project the feeling that they cannot be bought nor borrowed. The respect that people hold for God, they will be share with the minister whom they think to be directly under God's leadership. Some ministers who have accomplished spiritual feats for God, even though they might have worked in overalls beside laity, have lived and acted in such a way that everyone felt they were different, and that they were, of a truth, God's men.

If a minister is to be conscious of a close, positive divine leadership in his life, his relationship with God must be intimate. He must be convinced that God has chosen him personally to do a separate and different work for Him.

On the day that Chairman Peter stopped a prayer meeting so that the apostles might choose a replacement for Judas, he simply said, "Judas by transgression fell, that he might go to his own place." This was not the place God had ordained for him, but since he refused to fill the God-ordained place, he made another place for himself. He had a part in this ministry and apostleship, but "his bishoprick let another take." (See Acts 1:15-25.)

It is impossible for a preacher to be strongly conscious of divine leadership unless he feels that God's choice in his ministerial call was just as personal as Matthew's was on the day that Jesus stopped at his tax table. He must humbly feel that he personally has "come to the kingdom for such a time as this" (Esther 4:14). He has a unique service to render, a definite plan of his God to perform. No one else can do what God has meant for him to do. Every day is but another opportunity to render that service. Every hour draws him nearer the completion of the task; every minute is but one more step toward his goal. Every lost bit of time takes away from his life's program and leaves it, to that degree, unfinished.

In all of God's great plan there will be a missing link, a nook not perfected, if anyone fails to fill his place. There is no time to waste, no place to stop, no room to whine. God's program is big. It is full, and each one is a part of it. The Great Designer ordained each life at a specific time for a specific purpose.

If Christ is the door, the minister is the doorkeeper to open or close it for others. If Christ is the light of the world, the prophet is the bearer of that light to the ends of the earth. If Christ is the vine, the preacher is a fruit-bearing branch that draws life from that vine. If Christ is the bread of life, the minister is to break it to feed those who hunger. If Jesus is the truth, the pastor is the truth-bearer, the declarer and expounder of the truth. If Christ is the bright and morning Star, the minister's job it is to brush aside the clouds that veil His beauty from the world, that humanity may see and live forever. The person who would be led of God must feel the glory of this truth, that he is an indispensable part of the great plan and program of God.

This call and direction leads to the death of the self-life.

No minister can ever feel completely the rule of the Spirit in his life until self has abdicated the throne of his life.

The pioneers of the Pentecostal message are a good example of utter surrender. S. D. Stogner left a small clay hill farm in East Texas, loaded all he had in a covered wagon, and went out to an unfriendly world to preach the gospel. When his oldest girl grew ill, he trusted God with her until her dying breath. The feeling of the community, the treatment from sinners, and the threats of those who hated him were not pleasant to endure, but he had done what he believed to be the will of God for himself and his family.

One spring day a mob stood outside with a rope, promising to hang him if he prayed for a dying woman inside the house. His calm decision was that he had come as the pastor of the family, and if they requested prayer, he would pray, though it meant his life. Here was a man under authority, a man led of God. Self and convenience was not the idea here. If he could so ably face the very destruction of his body, then self-life itself must have already surrendered. Has this stringent note been lost?

The cry of the apostle condemns us, "That I may know him, and the power of his resurrection, and the fellowship of his sufferings, being made conformable unto his death" (Philippians 3:10). The passion to die to self, so strongly implied here and so aptly illustrated by Paul's great life, is fast becoming a lost passion. The strength of good soldiers is being wasted by good incomes and comfortable surroundings.

A communist once sneered when he was witnessed to. "Christ," he said, "died upon His cross, but you preachers come along and get fat on it." Too many times this is true. There is no doubt that more dying is needed—the death of the self-life. It is very easy to promote self under the guise of Christ, but what will the judgment reveal? Wood, hay, and stubble can fill a life (I Corinthians 3:12). Many times a minister has been content to receive a complimentary reward here from people rather than let Christ have the glory now and, in consequence, receive a much greater reward later at His dear hand.

Paul stated that part of his ministry was an attempt to fill up what was lacking in the suffering of Christ (Colossians 1:24). He could add nothing to the Atonement. When Jesus said, "It is finished," He took care of every item of redemption. But the grand old story needs a teller, and the teller is never convincing unless he lives the story that he is telling. So it seems that in every generation, and within the conscious notice of all living in that generation, Calvary must be reenacted.

The story of Calvary, however much it means to the minister, remains nothing more than an episode of history to many until they see its shadow fall across a life near to them and they witness the death of the self-life there. Why the great success of the apostle Paul? How was he able to bring so sharply the claims of the Cross to bear upon his hearers? Perhaps it was because that in his preaching and living they saw daily a crucifixion. It was not hard for them to believe one had died outside Jerusalem, when they daily saw one die in their midst.

Some years ago, a preacher was upon the cross of rejection in his church. Their treatment of him had reached such a degree that he was advised to leave, which he eventually did, without malice and with as much grace as he was able under the circumstances. He made a prized statement during a conversation prior to his leaving that church: "I feel that there are some things about Christianity that these people do not know. I doubt that they will ever experience them until they have had an example of Calvary. I think they need to witness a crucifixion, and I believe the Lord called me here to die." Calvary in Holy Writ is one thing, but Calvary lived out is another. Who will show the world Calvary in this generation?

When self is still proudly living and enthroned in the life of a preacher, the results are only too apparent. Who has not observed that preachers can be the most vengeful, cold-hearted, judgment-rendering people of God's creation? The proud and unsubdued self-life is behind these carnal manifestations. It is impossible for the selfish preacher to know the true leading of God. In fact, he is in a very dangerous position.

When someone recognizes and confesses his sinful self-centeredness, he has the mercy of God. But the self-life that clothes itself in its own righteousness and justifies its actions under the banner of godly zeal, receives no mercy. It is without repentance. It is blind and does not see itself, and therefore cannot repent. It is the kind that coldly watched Jesus die. It is hard for the person who is under domination of the self-life to know his real condition.

Job was a good man, but he had to die to self. He grandly survived material loss, but when his friends attacked his personal righteousness, that was quite another matter. In the charges and countercharges, the personal pronouns "I" and "me" were used almost two hundred times. Job finally had to reach the point where he was able to say, "I abhor myself, and repent in dust and ashes" (Job 42:6).

There is a power the Christians
Well may fear,
More powerful far than inborn sin
And to the heart more dear.
It is the power of selfishness,
The proud and willful "I."
And ere my Lord can live in me,
My very self must die.

When a preacher does not crucify self, he cannot hope to be God's man in the sense that he is led of God. When self sits upon the throne of the preacher's heart, it is small wonder that some commit adultery in thought or deed, become selfish and greedy for money, grow dictatorial and power mad, lust for honor that comes from people, and seek not honor that comes from God.

Some preachers sincerely strive all their lives to build great churches and never realize that the secret of success is growing great people. This is a work of the Spirit, and only a spiritual person can bring it about, with the help of God. People become truly great or remain obviously small in proportion to the esteem they give to self. If a person lives for self, provides for self, and saves self, he will die alone. Humans are not inherently great within themselves.

The cause that a person embraces will force him upward or drag him to the lowest depths. George Washington would have scarcely been heard of in history had it not been for the noble cause of freedom he espoused. The great cause of freedom lifted him from the small life he might have followed. Of course, the lifting did not take place until he had first given up himself and judged the cause to be greater than himself.

Along life's way there are sometimes people who, as a great Puritan, "have the strength of ten because their heart is pure." At the core of their being is the mammoth strength of unselfishness. It is impossible to crush such people. No one is strong until he is strong of heart and purpose. The real personal battles against sin and the devil are not fought in the church or in the community, but in the most secret chambers of a person's soul.

A singer once came before a great musical artist to be auditioned. A friend of the artist who happened to be present was tremendously impressed by the marvelous talent displayed by the singer and was extremely disappointed when the artist bluntly turned the singer down. Upon being questioned, the artist replied, "She lacks something. You might call it pathos, depth, or something else. What she needs is to have her heart broken, and then she will be able to really sing."

"The sacrifices of God are a broken spirit: a broken and a contrite heart, O God, thou wilt not despise" (Psalm 51:17). It is strange, however, that when God extends His chastening hand in order to kill the self-life, at once something goes to the defense of self. The self is justified and excused—dragged as it were from the very casket with water dashed in its face. A person is prone to preserve self, even under the most trying circumstances. But a minister should emulate the great example of Christ, who did not open His mouth when attacked. Christ's command to deny self is seemingly hard to obey.

One of the characteristics of self is that it attempts to own things in this world. Of course, real ownership in this life is a myth. Job admitted as much when he said, "Naked came I out of my mother's womb, and naked shall I return thither" (Job 1:21). Nevertheless, this attempt at ownership brings the greatest worry. The wise steward knows that God owns it all and that he is only an administrator on God's estate for a little while. The prudent pastor knows that he is an undershepherd and that the church is God's, which He purchased by His blood. When a person claims nothing as his own but his sins, he has no worries. How can some crack up over a world he is dead to? How can he break himself over a church that he does not hold to be his own? Self is the culprit often hidden behind work, motives, drives, and dreams.

The early Christians did not allow self to be their master. They owed allegiance only to Jesus Christ, and consequently, when all of their goods were taken from them and they were driven into the deserts and catacombs, they did not give up. They had lost nothing they had ever really owned. They were dead, and their lives were hidden in Christ. These were the kind of people who, in New Testament days, were truly led by the Spirit.

The call of God leads into a daily life that is hidden in Christ. This identification with Christ cannot transpire or endure unless the preacher is a person of prayer. Of all things the minister should not neglect prayer, but sadly, this seems to be one of the most glaring deficiencies. As a whole, Pentecostal ministers pray far more than the average layperson, but even at that, often it is not enough, nor is it the kind of praying that furthers the intimate spiritual relationship that the preacher needs with his Lord if he expects to be led by Him.

The preacher, of course, prays in public service. He usually leads the prayer, his voice being heard above the others. There are times in the prayer meeting when the weight of the service and other pending events prods him to fervency in prayer. The family man is careful to see that there is prayer with his children at night and in the morning before they leave the house. In this, however, he should be aware of the short endurance of the younger members of the family, and many times even the most conscientious man feels that prayer might be more of a ritual than a purposeful approach to God. The preacher will also pray in the discharge of his ministerial duties. In the course of a full day of pastoral work, he will likely pray in several homes or hospital rooms or with people who come to him for counsel. He will be called on for public invocations in many and varied observances. These appointments are merely functional appearances most of the time, in which the pomp and procedure of the occasion is prone to carry more weight than the gesture toward godly recognition.

There will be times in a preacher's life when the pressure of responsibility, whether it comes in the form of church troubles or simply weighty decisions, will drive him to his knees for seasons of prayer. This is good, and no minister could survive long if he did not exercise the sacred privilege of the inner sanctum. The tragedy is that the prayer rendezvous usually lasts only as long as the crisis, and then he is back again to a largely spiritless routine of duty.

The average preacher does pray. He prays through the day inwardly and secretly as various needs and oppressive thoughts come into his mind. But this is only snatch praying, a fleeting grasp for God's hand and then a preoccupied turning to other things just as quickly and abstractly. A lack of strong and fertile communion with God will be reflected in the prayer habit of the congregation where the minister holds forth. More than one good pastor has noticed that if he wants his people to really pray, he must pray himself. No leader can lift a congregation higher than himself.

This type of praying is, of course, better than nothing. It will probably exceed the praying of the average layperson, but it is not enough if the minister is to be strongly led by the Spirit. It will not hide him away in Christ. A spasmodic, clumsy, heartless approach to God will never lead the minister to greater Christian commitments, the lack of which is one of the great danger points of a careless preacher's life.

When we search the dark list of the fallen, we will find that they staggered in their Christian life when they came to the place of ease. When they tried to convince themselves that they had arrived, they failed. Preachers who have heavy loads on their backs usually do not fall into sin. It is the minister who refuses to accept the challenge for greater endeavors who is left behind to be overtaken by the hounds of hell. The person who does not sincerely seek God in the daily channels of a settled prayer life will not feel the claims of God laid hard against the door of his heart. He will not be stirred strongly by the possibilities of yet another project well done.

The usual round of ministerial praying will not deepen a life or cause it to grow up into the stature of Christ. The prayerless preacher has an earthliness about him that clings. He does not bear the image of the invisible. He does not leave the impression of being under authority. His ministry is arrested, enjoying no outstanding triumphs, knowing no progress either in the church he presently pastors nor in the size of pastorates that he migrates to.

Functional and dutiful praying will perhaps drag a minister through one day after another, but it leaves him without a love for the lost. A passionate concern for the unsaved comes only through association with the One who came "to seek and to save that which was lost" (Luke 19:10). Christ's passion for souls and concern for the lost will not belong to the preacher until he has taken Christ's yoke upon him in the closet with the closed door. Learning of Him must take place at His feet. There have been many "Martha" preachers who are encumbered about with many things but comparatively few who, like Mary, have chosen the better part. (See Luke 10:40-42.)

A mediocre prayer life results in a willingness to let things go that should be seized with a firm hand. Departments drag, and there is no mental energy or spiritual courage to activate them. Personal problems need to be dealt with, yet they remain week after week because the individual is not spiritually directed enough to dare lay a hand on them. One who does not really pray will not witness the Spirit of the Lord coming upon him as did Samson when he was challenged.

The press of the years, the circling weekends, and the endless need of promotion dry up the natural well, if the preacher has not sought to dig out the well that is to be within him, springing up into everlasting life. No one will persist in a given pastorate unless he has a continual endowment of power from on high. Perhaps that accounts for the frequent changes in pastorates that some preachers make.

Some things are hard to accomplish when promoting and leading a church to be a spiritual driving force in the community. Some hindering situations do not yield readily to prodding and suggestions. In time, natural courage will crumble with the fatigue of human setbacks. Only the spiritual leadership that comes through prayer will keep the pastor on his feet and coming back for another try.

Placid, half-hearted prayer efforts can be deceiving even to the preacher himself. They furnish enough initiative to do the ordinary duties of the day, but nothing more. There is no extra thrust to claim greater areas for God. No preacher will rise above the ordinary in his ministry until he rises first in his prayer habits. The world of things, pleasures, and self-gratification effectively hems in the preacher unless the extra impetus of prayer blasts him through these restraining influences and into the extraordinary. Mediocre praying colors the spiritual judgment of a person to a dirty shade of gray, so that it is impossible to see sharply and clearly. As a result, the minister cannot see the wickedness of neglect and the coldness of loveless relationships with God. Weakness is hidden, for only when a person comes into contact with God in all His power and radiant holiness does he come to know his own limitations. Ordinary praying will not bring him to this place.

Many a preacher has followed the dull round of days without spiritual perception, not knowing that the real power had departed from him until some Delilah duped him or other enemies had forever put his eyes out. The failures of Pentecostal preachers are most always prayer failures. When there is a failure in public or private, it is usually because of a failure first in the prayer closet. Most of the things that blight a ministry, crush a heart, and delay the work of God would not happen if prayer is offered as it should be.

Jesus' method of receiving divine communion and leadership while here on earth was prayer. The night before He chose His disciples, He prayed all night. He extended Himself for divine leadership through prayer. Can mortals do otherwise? He took for granted that those who would dedicate themselves to carry on His work would pray. So He said, "When you pray . . ." instead of, "If you pray . . ." (See Matthew 6:5-7.) He knew that neither the apostles nor anyone else could execute His plan and purpose upon this earth unless they were people of prayer. His great life and example taught the disciples the value of prayer.

The disciples sought and found Him one morning as He was praying. The setting indicates that they must have waited until He finished. His powerful praying awed them, and they felt impelled to petition Him. They did not ask Him to teach them to work miracles. They did not ask Him to teach them to preach. Rather, when they saw what prayer did for and through Jesus Christ, they valued it above all other attributes or activities of the Lord's life. Let us catch the earnest desire of that hopeful request, "Lord, teach us to pray." This should be the preacher's prayer. (See Luke 6:12-19; 11:1-4.)

Regular, persistent, heartfelt prayer affords the opportunity for the preacher to confess his sins. The broom of prayer brushes away the dust of deceit and enables the preacher, as the minutes pass, to become more and more honest with himself and his God. In time, he comes to his individual sins and weaknesses. As the

Spirit probes about his heart, and as the Lord encourages and urges him on, he at last is able to face them squarely as they are and confess them.

There is no permanent relief from sins until he sees them as personal, until he recognizes them as sin and not simply as mistakes and weaknesses, until he names the sin by its natural name. This is where the flesh shrinks back and would have a person pray around it or over it, but again and again the Holy Ghost lends the preacher in the closet, until at last he names it for what it actually is. Perhaps it was lust, covetousness, hatred, or some other poison to his soul; but, at last, when he names and confesses it, he pulls off the cover. It is now out in the open as acknowledged sin, and God can deal with it, forgive it, and help the preacher to overcome it. Only closet praying, however, will bring this about.

People do not commit adultery on the spur of the moment. In their daydreams, in their secret moments, in the chamber of their souls they begin their horrible descent. Over the months, and perhaps the years, they exist on merely ministerial functional praying. They do not have the strong winds of the prayer closet to blow away the cobwebs of blindness and allow them to see that their feet are beginning to take hold on the steps of hell.

Regular, persistent, heartfelt praying brings to the preacher's attention the many blessings of his life. He comes to see the true values of life and is made to feel that of all people he is blessed the most. This lends strength to his ability to withstand discouragement. Self-pity is the favorite tool of Satan, and he uses it most often on those who have not been led by the Spirit through prayer into the vast conservatories of God's blessing.

Thankful, praise-filled people never give up when Satan assaults them. They have counted their blessings and feel that, no matter what happens to them, they still have received more blessings than they deserve.

Regular, persistent, heartfelt praying keeps the preacher softened and tempered by the Spirit so that he can obey Christ's commands relative to praying for his enemies; and those who have tried it can guarantee that it works. He asks for grace to love them and to do good to them. Perhaps less than ten percent of all Christians obey this command. It is a sure, certain way to get rid of one's enemies. Why is it not used more often? Suffice it to say that only spiritual people will obey this command, because only spiritual people can. The carnal mind is not subject to the law of Christ, and neither indeed can it be. (See Romans 8:7.)

Enemies hurt the preacher's influence and hinder the progress of God's work. But the preacher is entirely unable to deal with them on a spiritual level unless he is a person of prayer. The preacher does not need people against him, he needs them with him, but year after year he keeps his antagonists unless he humbles himself through prayer to walk the road of love and forgiveness. This he will never do unless he prays, for no one can truly be led of God unless he is a person of prayer.

The preacher who is led of the Spirit comes to see that if he has results or success, they stem from Christ Himself and not from the preacher's ability. This feeling so lays hold of him that he largely divorces himself from personal responsibility for success or failure. Neither possibility is his paramount concern. He knows that his first responsibility is to do God's will faithfully in all sincerity. The results are beyond him, since it is "God that giveth the increase" (I Corinthians 3:7). He can only plant and water. This attitude saves the minister much fretting over circumstances that the devil would have him to believe mean the ruin of all his labor. It comforts him when Satan would destroy his peace by accusing him of personal responsibility for failure when he has done his very best.

The mature, broken, Spirit-led minister is slow to judge any circumstance as a failure. He has been awed too many times by the marvelous success of failure to fear it. He has worshiped too many hours personally at the feet of the world's greatest apparent failure. He knows that the carnal man cannot evaluate the economy of God, for he has seen God too often take the weak things and make strength, the foolish things and construe wisdom, the nothings and secure triumph over absolutes. His Lord chose the manger, the borrowed boat, the given cloak, the charity of society, and a borrowed tomb. He took the lowest and weakest in all things, condescending and stooping lower than the angels, lower than the lowest class to the role of servant, and then lower still in His obedience to death. Yet He triumphed!

The preacher who has denied self feels the kinship of Paul, who learned contentment in any state, for he knew that ultimately he would win. His last hours were spent in prison with filth, lice, and rodents for companions. Only Luke was with him. The churches he had labored so hard to establish had turned against him. Demas had departed to Thessalonica, "having loved this present world." (See II Timothy 4:10.) There was little to divide of the old preacher's meager belongings after his head had been severed. Yet in his last letter to his young preacher son in the gospel he looked expectantly into the sunrise instead of the sunset. He spoke of a crown, of a faith kept, and of a battle well fought. No doubt the world judged him a failure, but time renders quite another verdict, so that today everyone is arrested by the marvelous success of that failure. The Spirit-led person who has renounced self understands this, and thus much of his anxiety is taken away. He has assurance that in Christ there is not the remotest possibility of absolute, final failure.

One minister saw this assurance portrayed vividly in a statement that Missionary Verner Larsen made to workers in Colombia in 1957. As he stood before men who daily hazarded their lives for the gospel, who at times knew the pinch of hunger, and who had helped weep over some of their own brethren whose lives had been taken, he simply said, "Jesus will never fail you."

The simplicity and honest belief in what he was saying lent the statement its weight. The Spirit-led, self-renounced minister has so sunk himself down into Christ until he knows that even apparent failure can lead only to success and that it will fall out to the furtherance of the gospel.

This mature faith gives the preacher a persistence and steady drive that accomplishes much more than the erratic zeal which springs from human strength and ego. "Come with me, and see my zeal for the LORD," said Jehu to Jehonadab, as he invited him aboard his chariot (II Kings 10:16). This was all well and good, so long as there was a bloody project to take care of. It is hard at times to distinguish between "the zeal of thy house" and "my zeal" in the heat of a crisis-laden crusade. Alas, "my zeal" was not enough to carry Jehu all the way, for it is written of him,

"But Jehu took no heed to walk in the law of the LORD God of Israel with all his heart" (II Kings 10:31). He had carried out the furious driving and the uncompromising slaughters with the impetus of "my zeal," which in the end left his heart unchanged.

There is a zeal that gets much religious work done but is not of God. Much of the work is not done for God's glory, nor is it initiated by the Spirit. After building mammoth structures, both in mortar and organization, some preachers have fallen prey to many sins that lie in wait for the unbroken. We should never forget that the sacrifices of God are a broken spirit and a broken and contrite heart.

The Spirit-led preacher knows the secret of the abiding life as set forth by Jesus in John 15. He was only a few hours away from the crucifixion. On His way to the bloody sweat of Gethsemane, Jesus paused in the Kidron Valley. Now He would speak only a few more words with His disciples before His death. The words He chose surely must be important ones. Let us note John 15:2-7:

"Every branch in me that beareth not fruit he taketh away; and every branch that beareth fruit, he purgeth it, that it may bring forth more fruit. Now ye are clean through the word which I have spoken unto you. Abide in me, and I in you. As the branch cannot bear fruit of itself, except it abide in the vine; no more can ye, except ye abide in me. I am the vine, ye are the branches: he that abideth in me, and I in him, the same bringeth forth much fruit: for without me ye can do nothing. If a man abide not in me, he is cast forth as a branch, and is withered; and men gather them, and cast them into the fire, and they are burned. If ye

abide in me, and my words abide in you, ye shall ask what ye will, and it shall be done unto you."

Clearly, Jesus pointed out the source of all production and made it clear that no one can produce the fruit of the Spirit except by the Spirit. The same "sap" or Spirit that is Jesus Christ must flow through the preacher's entire concept and work. Otherwise, he may produce something, but it will not be the fruit of the Spirit, and it will neither be lasting nor acceptable before God.

God will not even accept human righteousness that is not a product of the spiritual sap but counts it as "filthy rags" (Isaiah 64:6). If a preacher can produce the type of life he is now living or promote the program he is presently promoting without sincere prayer and the flow of the Spirit, then neither his life nor his work, however beautiful and promising they may seem, are acceptable in the eyes of God. Human efforts cannot produce a spiritual good. Jesus himself declared, "That which is born of the flesh [conceived and initiated by human effort] is flesh; and that which is born of the Spirit [conceived and initiated by the Spirit] is spirit" (John 3:6). While in context this verse speaks of the new birth, it contains a principle of general application.

The branch must abide in the vine (the trustful, broken, selfless life) if it is to produce fruit that our Lord will accept. The divine "sap" of the Spirit must flow through all intentions, motivate all activities, and lend strength to all projects, if the end result is something truly born of God. This stated fact of the spiritual life is not an imposed limitation on work but a simple law of life that we must work with gladly if our work is to abide until the day of

His coming. "Except the LORD build the house, they labour in vain that build it" (Psalm 127:1). Unless the preacher gives Christ His rightful place of centrality in his life and work, he will come to the judgment seat of Christ perhaps with a saved soul but with a tragically wasted life. All other ground is sinking sand.

Zeal that would prompt a person to give his body to be burned, unless sanctified by God, is nothing. Benevolence that would bestow all of a person's goods, unless given as a product of the divine motive that dwelt also in Jesus Christ, profits nothing. Wisdom and eloquence equaling that of humans and angels produce exactly nothing if the flow of the Spirit does not move them outward. Abilities that promote self-interest, instead of ministering to the needs of others, are inadequate. What tricks a heart can play! "The heart is deceitful above all things, and desperately wicked: who can know it?" (Jeremiah 17:9).

The secret of a worthwhile ministry is to abide in the Lord. The essence of divine leadership is simply abiding in Christ. When the preacher abides in Him, he comes to know Him through relationship and experience. He develops a calm, trustful attitude based on the sure knowledge that it is "not by might, nor by power, but by my spirit, saith the LORD" (Zechariah 4:6). He comes to know that as long as he is in God's will, is faithful in his discharge of daily duty, and keeps the Spirit flowing through his life by prayer and daily communion, he will produce fruit. There is but one God, and He is the producer of all good. "Without me ye can do nothing," but "I can do all things through Christ which strengtheneth me" (John 15:5; Philippians 4:13).

The greatest, safest, and most productive thing a preacher can do is to abide in Christ. This means to rest upon His ability, since the flesh cannot render a spiritual product. There is no other choice if one is to do God's work. He must sink himself down into the Christ life, eating of His flesh and drinking of His blood, letting the sap of the Spirit flow from the true vine right out to the end of all of his efforts. When the preacher ceases from the strain of his own abilities and relaxes himself in the divine purpose and ability of God, he will eliminate much of the strain of the ministry.

Jesus asked His followers to "consider the lilies how they grow" (Luke 12:27). Well, how do they grow? Is it with undue strain and anxiety that they lift themselves with great effort above the muck of their environment? Has anyone ever passed at night by the lily pond and heard wretched groans and sighs issuing from it as the lilies wrestled mightily with the circumstances of surrounding muck? No, Jesus spoke of the lilies in terms of trust. He used them as an example to show that certain laws of nature worked for them, and all they did was to follow a process of growth provided for them by the kind wisdom of a loving God. Out of weakness (muck and ugliness) they are made strong and lovely.

Happy is the preacher who comes to see, before he has ruined his health, that the church is not an institution so much as it is a living organism. It carries within itself provisions for its own growth and production. Because of sickness in the local group, there are times when it grows slowly, or not at all. But through God, even the sick church has the mysterious ability to heal herself if cared for discreetly and fed wisely by a Spirit-led pastor. This healing might take years, but the mature preacher discerns this and does not try to force the healing or to impose a false growth. He knows how the lilies grow. He knows that if he can lead the congregation to Christ and to an abiding trust, the sap will flow, bringing with it all that is needed.

The preacher who has this insight will content himself to cooperate daily with God—comforting, encouraging, loving, being kind—knowing that God has more equity, by far, in the church than he does and that surely He will resurrect it.

The church of the living God is not built with cold, man-made programs, though God does sanctify them for His use if we work with Him, but the church grows from within through the Spirit of the living God. Many preachers are disappointed and baffled because no progress comes, in spite of all of their sincere and eager efforts. Aside from spiritual leadership, a minister should not impose his will and programs upon the successful church. It is the body of Christ. It grows as the lilies grow. If this approach to overseeing the church seems to remove personal initiative and aggressiveness, we must remember, in the final analysis, that unless God builds the house, they labor in vain who build it. (See Psalm 127:1.)

In truth, this approach does not minimize work, but it simply follows the pattern of the New Testament church, which was so successful. Mark 16:20 describes this working arrangement: "And they went forth, and preached every where, the Lord working with them, and confirming the word with signs following."

A minister once wrote: "I am sorry to say that I worked many long, hard years sincerely and faithfully for God. I tried very hard, only to see more than one church fail under my pastorate. I noticed that there were some preachers who seemed to know a secret. It appeared that

134

everything they put their hand to was a success. I longed so much to find this secret, and in my efforts I talked to them about it. They did not seem to know the secret themselves, but it was apparent to me that they had gotten hold of something that I had not come across. I knew that I worked as hard as and sometimes harder than they did. I don't know how it came about, but whether in one day or over a period of time, it dawned upon me that there was a vast difference between working with God and working for God."

The secret of the New Testament church was that the apostles worked with God and not just for God. The church grew as the lilies grow, in perfect harmony with the laws of the spiritual life. The sap flowed and the branches simply rested in the vine, not in any way trying to exhibit themselves but swallowed up in the intent of the whole organism.

The same minister went on to say: "I cannot say that I am particularly proud of any accomplishment that might seem to have come my way since this discovery, but I am warmly comforted by the fact that what has transpired has been the natural product of God through me, that my life has been the will of God, lived out, and that I have been so greatly honored to work with God instead of remotely for Him. I have treasured sweetly the calm, contented, fruitful years since this discovery, glorying in the truth: 'He that dwelleth in the secret place of the most High shall abide under the shadow of the Almighty' (Psalm 91:1). I can witness that this 'abiding' has taken much fear and worry out of my ministry."

The wise man has said, "To every thing there is a season, and a time to every purpose under heaven"

(Ecclesiastes 3:1). This is a law with which no one would argue. The seasons come and go in their turn and time, the birds migrate accordingly, night and day follow in continuous sequence, the tide ebbs and flows, and the cycles of life in a thousand ways verify the orderliness of God's creation. This natural rhythm is not confined to material or inanimate objects, but there is an unheard pulse that beats out the great purpose of God throughout His creation.

Just as God established order in creation, He also wishes for a person's life to be rhythmic and musical, not tumultuous and self-disappointing. There is a place for everything and everything in its place; a time for everything and everything done in its time. This is not the heartlessness of mere machinery but the very perfection of ease and enjoyment. Accepting the abiding life entails the least possible waste, divides all burdens equally, and makes the wheels of life go steadily and correctly.

The human race seemingly has lost its marching step, and now each goes at his own pace, wildly, confusedly, blindly, while the spirit of panic has displaced the spirit of peace. But for the person called to be the shepherd of God's flock, this should not be. He should know that if he abides in Christ's will, work, purpose, and Spirit, all things must work together for his good. Even when called upon to execute the difficult beats of life, he confidently rests his soul on God's purpose, letting love and goodwill clothe all he contacts.

The New Testament church demonstrates the importance of divine timing and of working with God. It moved through sixty years of sacred history as a great symphony tuned to the wavelength of God's will. The Holy Ghost was given when "the day of Pentecost was fully come."

Had the Samaritan woman come an hour later, she would have missed Jesus at Jacob's well. Peter went to the housetop to pray at just the right time. Philip arrived on the Gaza road on schedule. Paul cast a demon out of the young girl on the appointed day.

Let us notice the leading and the timing of the Spirit in the life of Paul. In his second missionary journey he came to Phrygia and Galatia, but there the Spirit restrained him and told that he could not go to Asia. Departing from there, he came to Mysia and started to Bithynia, but once again the Holy Ghost told him no. It was not yet time for the great Ephesian revival. God had great intentions for that city, but the time had not yet come for Him to show His hand there.

Paul might have been disappointed by the delay. He had no way of knowing, however, that two years from then this city would be the seat of one of the greatest revivals the world has ever known. This revival was to be purely Pentecostal in practice and in experience. It was to clean many homes of things not conducive to godly living, spark such fervor in the hearts of converts that in an incredibly short time it could be said that "all they which dwelt in Asia heard the word" (Acts 19:10). The church at Ephesus mothered the seven churches of Asia Minor, referred to in Revelation, plus many others in the great Phrygian Valley, and it all came about exactly on time.

Just as important, God's church in the earth today is right on time. The United Pentecostal Church International has come to the kingdom for such a time as this.

This practice of the abiding life, this impulse of divine leadership, is not always initiated by tremendous revelations, though Pentecost ceases to be thoroughly Pentecost

137

when the miraculous is doubted. This Spirit-led ministry is to be a normal existence of the Pentecostal minister. It is nothing more than what Paul described as having the mind of Christ.

There is sometimes in every life a quandary about knowing the will of God. Perhaps the simplest way to be always in God's will for the future is to practice each day what we know to be the will of God in all things for that day. A daily life of trustful obedience in all things gives assurance that when tomorrow arrives, along with it will come the knowledge of His will for that day.

Once again, let us look at the divine rhythm of life. For instance, a man and a woman who have been married awhile and have lived in mutual love and confidence with one another, begin to think alike and actually begin to resemble one another. Many times they will both make almost the same comment on a certain subject not previously discussed. They begin to operate more or less on the same wavelength.

So it is with the Spirit. In Christ, the church becomes bone of his bone and flesh of his flesh. The Spirit-led minister who has sunk himself down into the abiding Christ life does not agonize daily to know the will of God in all particulars. He has the mind of Christ. He thinks like God so much that his first impression will often be the will of God. He is in step with the infinite, in harmony with the divine law, caught up in a spiritual impetus.

Through the ages people have caught the throb of a holy call and heard the beat of marching feet. Moses refused to be called the son of Pharaoh's daughter, choosing rather to suffer affliction with the people of God than to enjoy the pleasures of sin for a season. He left the palace to march in another band, to another beat. He was forty years off in his timing at first, but since he "endured, as seeing him who is invisible," everything turned out all right. (See Hebrews 11:27.) He came to the sunset of one of the most worthwhile lives the world has ever known.

Happy is the preacher who discovers that he is not a bulldozer designed to shove program after program through his church at his own discretion, but that he is a cultivator of God's husbandry (tilled field), and that he may plant and another may water, but it is God who gives the increase.

Good things done at the wrong time are not good. A good preacher coming at the wrong time for a revival is not good. Much of a person's work will be wasted if he does not catch the divine beat. There is a time to plant, to water, and to harvest; a time to speak, to be silent, to comfort, and to rebuke sharply. It is easy to say, "All things work together for good to them that love God." Many people stop in the middle of the verse, but it adds a stipulation: "to them who are the called according to his purpose." (See Romans 8:28.) Life is underscored by the great, eternal purpose of God, and if a minister will launch himself down into the abiding Christ life, there is no need for him to worry about anything. Growth will be as the lilies—relaxed, sure, and perfect.

Blessed is the preacher who learns to listen for the holy beat of God's will for each service. Even while the service progresses, while he hears the songs and testimonies with his ears, another part of him listens and reaches to find and feel the divine pulse and will of God. This procedure is no strain to him. For the broken, self-renounced, trusting preacher, it has become a way of life.

It is his loving Friend, with whom he has spent time and fellowship all week, that he now seeks to please in all things. He knows Him so well that he comprehends even the slightest gesture and impulse of the Spirit. He does not need a direct order. Having the mind of Christ, he anticipates and discerns the desire of the Spirit. To that church, the flow of the divine sap is not hindered, but in each service and in every instance it comes to bring whatever is needed, so the wounded are healed, the weak are nourished, and the presumptuous are restrained.

Such a minister not only knows God, but he knows people as well. To him has been given the greatest gift, though this type of person never uses it in such a way that anyone would be aware of it. It is the great gift that God promised Jacob long ago by the brook Jabbok: "For as a prince hast thou power with God and with men, and hast prevailed" (Genesis 32:28). Such a pastor has a wonderful way of bringing people and God together, so that the congregation is refreshed. The preacher will hide behind the Cross and wisely bring Christ to the center in all things.

Thrice blessed is the person who knows that "except the LORD build the house, they labour in vain that build it," and that it is "not by might, nor by power but by my spirit, saith the LORD."

8

The Minister and Special Services

Sometimes a preacher who preaches well does rather poorly in special services such as weddings, funerals, baptisms, and the administration of the Lord's Supper. Why is it that a good preacher who may have been preaching for some time still lacks the polish and direction he is expected to have relative to these public functions? It could be that he underestimates the importance of efficiency here. We should take care of this facet of the ministry, and do so with grace and thoroughness, for the honor of the office and for the sake of others.

There is a smoothness and dignity with which the minister can take care of these occasions. The Pentecostal preacher should not be one step behind preachers of any denomination in executing forthrightly any of the services for which his church may be responsible. A properly rendered service is like a well-served meal. It leaves behind a certain satisfaction and appreciation for the pastor who conducted it. People will drive out of their way, pay extra, and tip more freely in order to treat themselves to the respect and dignity of a well-served meal. They pay extra for the quiet atmosphere, the large cloth napkin, the plentiful silverware, and the decorum observed by those administering the service.

Likewise, the people of a congregation are thankful for a pastor who can confidently take care of the responsibilities of various special services. It is not stretching a point to say that the pastor owes it to his congregation to give proper service. At weddings and funerals there will be people of the community who would not ordinarily attend a Pentecostal service, and the members of the church will be hoping that the pastor is able to make a good impression for the church they love and support.

The Lord's Supper

One of the services usually conducted with only the church family is the Lord's Supper. In many cases, this ordinance is not administered as often as it should be, and when it is done, often not enough forethought is given. The degree of importance that we attach to an ordinance is contingent upon our theological interpretation of it. Pentecostals believe that this observance has its proper place and emphasis in our worship, so it should not be slighted. Sometimes the Lord's Supper is received poorly because the people did not properly prepare their hearts by a period of prayer beforehand. It is always best that the congregation know a week in advance that the following Sunday the Lord's Supper will be served. Without this prior knowledge, many will not be in the right spiritual attitude for it.

There are times that a congregation does not attain the proper degree of worship in the serving of communion because its administration is clumsy and poorly planned. The same thing happens when there is no follow-through of spiritual appreciation at the close of the service. I Corinthians 11:18-34 gives a glimpse of the malpractice of this service by the Corinthian church in the days of the apostles. Their pagan concepts of a religious supper were reflected in their feasting on this occasion and even making themselves drunk. Consequently, the apostle Paul gave them instructions relative to the solemnity and reverence that Christians should assume during this observance.

Even in Pentecost, different ministers place somewhat different theological emphasis upon the Lord's Supper. Some believe that the service itself effects a certain blessing. Some take advantage of its serving to pray for the sick, believing that it has certain merits relative to healing. Some pastors have had sincere members of their church ask for communion while on the sickbed or just before undergoing major surgery. Most ministers agree that, while the Lord's Supper is certainly effective to inspire faith and bestow comfort, its primary purpose is not physical healing. According to Matthew 26, it is a memorial to Christ's death. It reminds us that the blood of Jesus Christ is indeed efficacious for the remission of sins and the salvation of souls. Partaking of the Lord's Supper inspires faith to accept the Atonement and fills us with hope as we look forward to partaking of it with Christ at His second coming. The memory and blessing of this ordinance being what they are, the pastor should study and pray so that it will be beautiful, meaningful, and blessed.

How often should this service be administered? This is at the discretion of the pastor of the local church, as the Scriptures do not specify. It is wonderful that he has this leeway, and if he is wise, he will use it to a good advantage. There are occasions that can be further solemnized by the use of the Lord's Supper.

Some groups receive it every Sunday and even make this a point of contention with other groups who do not follow their practice. Should it be received every Sunday? Doing so would be all right if it would be received in the proper spirit. Paul commanded, however, for everyone examine himself prior to taking communion. How long should this examination take?

Some churches that receive communion every Sunday do not have enough variety in their worship to do without it. They lean upon it for a strong point of emphasis. Churches bereft of God's power have always resorted to a procedure that they could make beautiful and impressive. "The less Spirit, the more ritual" is usually the rule.

However, perhaps communion is not offered enough in many Pentecostal churches. It probably should be given more than once a year. Many churches close each quarter with a week of twenty-four hours per day of prayer chain, and the following Sunday they receive the Lord's Supper. This plan seems to work well, for it gives the congregation time for heart preparation. They feel more comfortable engaging in it since they have had time for preparation. Some have refused to participate, not because of harm they might do to themselves by receiving it unworthily, but because they felt it would degrade the worthy observance to partake of it with a cold heart. Such people should prepare themselves and be ready at any time to partake of communion.

Many ministers offer the Lord's Supper during the Sunday morning service. However, variety may be better, as variety is one of the characteristics of Pentecost. God Himself always has the right to order the service, and He has a way of making the service different, interesting and varied. The Lord's Supper can be served at the close of a Sunday evening service or in the middle of the week at the close of a Bible study devoted especially to the subject. Whenever it is given, we must not forget that Christ had a certain purpose in instituting it; thus, each time we receive it, each individual should find that purpose.

There is no set way to administer the Lord's Supper, and everyone can learn from one another. As we have mentioned, at times a sermon or a study should be given on the Lord's Supper, but this is not necessary every time it is received. As the pastor often pauses briefly before he baptizes a candidate in water to exhort on the merits of baptism, so it is fitting just before the reception of the Lord's Supper for the pastor to make a few forceful, appropriate remarks relative to it. Most of the time the very nature of communion deems that it should be served during the last part of the service. It is to be the climax, and nothing should supersede it.

Here are some recommendations as to procedure. First, it is almost superfluous to say that the table and equipment should be prepared beforehand. The fruit of the vine should be poured into the glasses and the bread placed in trays. In case more is needed, the container should be available so that the need can be taken care of speedily. It is fitting and impressive if the implements of the service are covered with a white cloth and remain before the congregation during the entire service preceding the serving.

The brethren who will assist the pastor should be briefed beforehand as to the procedure and can sit together. When they are called, they should come forward, two of them lifting and folding the covering. At this point, some find it a blessing to have the congregation read together I Corinthians 11:23-33, after which the bread is offered to the brethren who are serving. Before the serving of the fruit of the vine, Matthew 26:27-29 is read, and then the helping brethren are served.

As to the procedure by which to serve the congregation, each pastor will find what works best for the size of the congregation and what brings the most reverence into the service. Some congregations are served at the altar area, with just enough coming each time to fill it and then rising immediately and going back to their pews, so that others can come. Or the servers can move throughout the congregation. In larger gatherings, the men have been invited to the platform and front of the building, and the women have knelt at every other pew, so that the servers could move among them. The congregation can come forward in line, receiving the bread and the drink from two or more brethren who state the purpose of each emblem to those who come. After receiving the elements, they partake of them immediately, or choose for themselves a place of prayer and do not eat or drink until they feel within themselves that they are prepared to do so. This seems to give them a certain privacy and choice in one of the most sacred moments of the Christian life.

The occasion is such that it deserves to be closed with dignity and reverence. While people are still standing about the altar, an appropriate hymn or chorus should close the worship service.

The Wedding

Another special service that the pastor is called upon to execute is the wedding. Among all the varied services that are the pastor's responsibility, none is more important than the wedding. Considering the length of time the marriage is to endure, the importance that God attaches to it, and the children that will come from the union, it is a function to which the pastor should carefully attend.

Ministers do not have a direct command of God to perform a wedding ceremony. The scriptural instructions and the attention that God gives to marriage more than indicate, however, that it is most proper for a marriage to have the instruction of the minister and the blessing of the church upon it. The discerning pastor knows that the end to be sought is not the ceremony itself but a compatible and successful marriage. If there is no hope for this, the preacher has a right to refuse to perform the ceremony. No honest preacher should have a part in perpetuating heartbreak and homeless children.

Many books have been written to the bride and the groom, given instructions and listing responsibilities for each of them prior to the ceremony. But there are few instructions for the minister relative to his responsibilities before the marriage. This is unfortunate, since he should lay the groundwork for an easier adjustment for the young couple.

No minister can undo the effect of home life on those who are coming for marriage. For this reason, the good pastor prepares the youth of his congregation for marriage in the regular discharge of his pastoral teaching. He will find it desirable several times each year to teach on Pentecostal home life, pointing out the simple fundamentals of getting along well together. He will instruct parents in the good habits of spirituality within the home, encouraging family prayer and everyday honesty and kindness within the family.

Good homes beget good homes, and a church is no stronger than the home life of the families who attend. The interest the pastor has shown through the years in the young people of his congregation will largely determine whether they will bring their problems to him later in life once they are married. An aggressive youth program has its place in the successful marriages of young people in the local congregation, inasmuch as it enhances the possibility that, through healthy fellowship together, they will tend to seek out members of their own faith for marriage.

The pastor should hold from one to three prenuptial conferences with the couple who is anticipating marriage. If possible, this should be some weeks before the wedding. In settled church families, marriages on the spur of the moment are usually the exception. At the first conference, the minister and the couple should discuss the specific date of the wedding and check the calendars of the church and the pastor.

Either in that meeting or in one following, the pastor needs to discuss the true nature of marital love. It is not unusual for young people to feel that marital love comes already developed and matured with nothing more to be added. It is often a comfort to them later if they have been told that disappointments and temporary loss of zest for one another does not mean a failure in marriage but that they will grow more and more into a lasting love that will exceed their feeling for each other at the start.

The minister should point out to them some of the pitfalls of marriage and warn that human love can die unless it is cultivated and cared for. He should help the young couple realize that love grows from the fertile soil of trust, honesty, admiration, and compatibility. He should explain that during the first year of marriage the curiosity, adventure, and natural attraction that draw them to one another are nothing more than the scaffold around which they must build the real structure of lasting love. But if they do not conduct themselves during the first few months of marriage so as to inspire trust, honesty, and admiration in each other, they may be headed for trouble.

In one of these sessions, the minister should clearly point out the duties of the husband and the wife. He will need to prepare himself for these conferences so that they will be informative and unforgettable. It is vital that the couple decide in the minister's presence the respective roles of each of them in their life together, including how they will handle finances.

It is probably a good idea for the minister to give them a good, simple book on marriage and sex. Some feel that the minister should counsel them together on this subject. Others do not feel that this is appropriate. If they ask advice on this subject and both indicate they feel the need of such counsel, perhaps so. However, this is very unlikely. Inexpensive books are available that deal adequately with the subject from a Christian perspective. In privacy, a book will be more appreciated than an intrusion on the subject under awkward circumstances. It is quite all right for the pastor to speak to the young man as a friend if he feels that he needs to do so; and if such is deemed necessary, the pastor's wife can do so with the young woman.

In these sessions, the pastor should stress the imperative need of prayer and faithful church attendance. "Families that pray together stay together." In fact, at each session the pastor should have prayer with the couple before they leave.

The question arises with every minister, What should I do about marrying someone who has a living companion? Pentecostal brethren have different convictions regarding this problem. Some ministers do not marry anyone, regardless of the situation, if he or she has a living companion. Others will marry them based on an analysis of the past circumstances. If it is a scruple of a minister not to marry anyone with a living companion, his refusal will be understood as long as he is consistent in his decision. If he performs one ceremony and refuses another of similar circumstances, however, he opens himself for criticism.

The minister who performs marriage ceremonies should have some knowledge of the laws of the state in which the ceremony is performed. It is important to remember that these laws vary, and ignorance of the particulars can be very embarrassing. Some states require a waiting period of a certain number of days after the purchase of the license. Others require a certain number of witnesses before the marriage is valid. Of course, the minister should be careful how and where he signs the license. To be safe, it is best to take care of the signing and the mailing the same night as the wedding, if possible. More than one minister has either forgotten or misplaced the license.

In an area where there is more than one Pentecostal church and the youth of the various churches intermarry, occasionally there is the question of ethical considerations. If the couple is from two different churches, it is proper that the bride's pastor perform the ceremony. It is also proper that they attend the groom's church after marriage if he prefers to do so. If both of the young people are active Christians, the bride's pastor should invite the groom's pastor to assist him in the wedding. The pastor who is invited to assist may refuse kindly if he chooses, without anyone feeling affronted.

The couple may approach a minister who is pastor to neither of them. This is unusual, but if it should happen, the approached pastor should urge them to go to see their own pastor. He has no business to arrange a wedding where neither parties are members of his church. In order to show that he is acting in good faith, he should contact the couple's pastor as soon as possible, tell him of the approach made to him, and assure him that he urged the couple to go to their own pastor. No preacher should enter into the responsibility of another unless he is invited and the resident minister is the one who does the inviting. It should be made clear to any party who makes such an approach that such an arrangement is impossible. If the pastor, because of local church circumstances, would find it awkward to perform the ceremony and invites an outside minister to do it, that will be all right.

Inasmuch as the wedding is the high point of the couple's life and an emotion-filled event for the parents, the ceremony itself should be performed in the most gracious way. Many books offer instructions for a beautiful and solemn ceremony.

Often, the question of the fee comes into the mind of the minister. Should he receive fees from couples he marries? In general, the pastor should count the ceremony a part of his pastoral duty to a faithful member of his congregation. However, if must go out of town for the ceremony, it may be in order for the couple to offer a fee to cover extra expenses. If he marries a couple who are not members of his congregation, especially if they are not Pentecostal, he should feel no twinge of conscience at all in taking a fee for his service.

The thorough pastor does not quite feel that his duty in the wedding is discharged even after the signing of the license. There is at least one more thing that he can do. He should write a warm pastoral letter to the couple, expressing his fond hopes for them and once again assuring them that the safest marital route is by way of regular church attendance. He should promise them his prayers and help any time they have need of them.

The Funeral

Another time of special service for ministers is the funeral. There is no time in the life of a layperson when he will feel his need of the pastor's help, nor appreciate it any more, than at the sorrowful time of death. Bereavement is usually the greatest trial of life. It is so final and so lonely when those left behind come into naked contact with the awe and mystery of death. It is at this time that people sense strongly the need of someone whom they feel is more closely in touch with the unknown world beyond.

If they are not saved, there is no better time than this to begin a spiritual relationship with the bereaved family.

It is during such trials that grief breaks the heart and the soul moves toward God. For the moment, sinful inclinations spread their dark wings and depart, while the door of the heart is left ajar for kind words fitly spoken for Jesus. Many ministers can witness that they formed the greatest friendships of their ministry while ministering to people during the time of sorrow.

No matter how often the minister faces the scenes of sorrow, he should never become hardened or so used to grief that he cannot be touched with the feeling of other people's infirmity. Such an attitude is sure to show, either on the face or in the slighted service rendered.

The first thing to remember when a member of the congregation dies is to act promptly. Sometimes death comes while the pastor is by the family's side. The long vigils during which the pastor waits with a lonely family will be repaid in a thousand ways later on. If the sickness has been long and drawn out (and it is hard to predict the time of passage for the ill), the preacher will find it necessary to absent himself to take care of other matters and to obtain some rest for himself. In such situations, he should be sure to ask the family to call in case the patient takes a decided turn for the worse. When a call comes informing the pastor that the patient or the family needs him, he should, if at all possible, stop what he is doing and go to their side immediately.

His entrance into the scene of grief should be quiet and purposeful. In every way his approach should manifest kindness and concern. There might not be anything that he can say, but speech at this point is not so necessary. Just having the pastor there means so very much. After a short time, he can speak kind remarks about the loved one. If someone is overcome emotionally, it is well for the minister to take the lead in seeing that he or she is taken care of and that proper procedures are administered in case of fainting. Usually nothing more is needed than a cold, wet cloth and a place to lie down.

It is good for the minister to offer his help in contacting the doctor, funeral director, and relatives. It is not unusual for the family to desire that the minister go to certain absent members of the family and break the news gently to them. The minister should not leave the house until the first shock has passed and the family has calmed. He should not leave until he has called them together and prayed with them, shaken hands with all present, assured them that he will be back soon, and insisted that they contact him for any further information or need.

The family might become collected enough while the pastor is there to proceed with the secondary arrangements. However, he should not force this upon them. The pastor can kindly mention to them before he leaves, "There are some things that you will want to talk about relative to the funeral arrangements, but we do not have to speak of them just now if you had rather not. I can come back in a few hours, and perhaps you will feel more like talking about them then." Many times they will say, "No, let's talk about them now." And of course, in such cases he will go right ahead and make the secondary arrangements while he is there.

The first thing to decide upon is the date and hour of the service. In this arrangement the family, the funeral director, and the pastor must all agree. Once in a while the funeral director may have another service scheduled, so the first time picked by the family will not be possible.

Almost never does the pastor have anything so important that he cannot be at the side of a faithful family at the most crucial time of their lives. If they never needed him before, they certainly need him then.

The pastor is wise to use his influence kindly and imperceptibly to schedule the funeral service sooner rather than later, provided that the family does not have to wait for the arrival someone who is a long distance away. They should allow ample time before the service for the death notice to appear in the local daily paper, if such is the practice in the community. Usually, if the decease has occurred in the night or early morning, the funeral service can occur on the afternoon of the second day following, or on the morning after that. Various factors, such as the arrival of relatives, sometimes enter in to cause the funeral services to be set a day or so later. Where the relatives are near and all other arrangements can be taken care of within thirty-six hours, there is no reason why the body cannot be committed without further delay. The minister is being a friend to the family by cautiously suggesting an earlier time. Delaying the service only prolongs the strain of the final farewell. No earthly good is done by long periods of waiting between the time of death and the final committal.

However, the final decision as to time will be the family's. In such matters the minister only stands by to serve and quietly suggest when he is needed.

The second thing to take care of in these arrangements is the place where the service will be held. There are typically four places to choose from: the home of the deceased, the church, the funeral home, and the cemetery. Few funerals are now held in the home, though this used to be a common practice. There are also fewer funerals conducted in churches than formerly. This, at first glance, might seem to indicate a declension in religious preference, but it has its merits.

To the relatives, the church is a place of comfort where distressing thoughts are put away for a little while. More than one person has admitted that for some time when he came to church, needing so much the healing touch of true, warm worship, he could not help but envision the casket that had been opened before the pulpit.

One dear family lost a fine young son and chose to have the funeral in the church. These good people had a prayer time for years in the church, but after the funeral this wonderful rendezvous in the church ceased. It pained them to enter the quietness of the sanctuary alone, for then thoughts crowded in upon them and they relived the funeral service for a long time.

There is another side to this matter, however. It may be that after the shock passes, the memory of the loved one is associated with the church more fully, thereby making a firmer tie to the institution that stood by them with comfort and help during the most trying hours of life. Again, this is a decision for the family to make.

The third thing the pastor must help the family decide is the selection of pallbearers. At times, men from the class that their loved one attended are chosen. If the deceased is an older person, the family sometimes prefer the grandsons or the nephews. The responsibility may be left with the pastor to get whomever he will from the church family. Whatever is done, it is often the minister's responsibility to contact the pallbearers, stating the time and the place of the funeral and carefully informing them to appear at the church or funeral home fifteen minutes before the service is to begin. They should be informed when and where to meet with the director, who will instruct them from there. After the service, the minister should shake hands with each of the pallbearers and convey to them his appreciation for their help.

When it comes to the order of the service, the family usually has little knowledge and feels that the minister will capably take care of it all very well. It is discreet to ask the family if they have any preference as to the songs sung. If they have any other preference, they will usually mention it at this time. It is fair to grant them this privilege, but the pastor should not leave the impression that helping to plan the service is a part of their responsibility.

There are some other chores that the minister may need to see about. One of them is seeing if they would like someone to remain with the body at night. In some areas of the country this is not practiced at all, while other families feel very keenly about it.

There are times also that the family is greatly helped by the minister's accompanying them in the selection of the casket and the choosing of the burial plot. Some families expect this of the minister. It is a good idea for the minister to be present while these arrangements are being made, since people are sometimes so broken by grief that they have a tendency to spend far beyond what is necessary or in keeping with their finances. The interested pastor will seek to protect them against a decision that would not be in their best interest. Not only are they grief-stricken, but they are thrust into unfamiliar surroundings and called upon to decide on variables of which they are unsure. Much of their insecurity is allayed if their pastor is present, though he may not say a word.

Whether or not the pastor is present is actually decided by the home and family circumstances. If the family has a firm sense of direction and a good background of sound judgment, the pastor will not feel so obligated as he might otherwise.

What are the duties of the funeral director? Procedures differ in various areas of the country, so if the minister is new to a certain locality it would be good for him to check everything out so there will be no awkward moments. Most of the undertakers secure information from the family about the deceased and a picture, which they file with the local paper. The information they gather will also be used to make the obituary that is given to the minister for the funeral service. The director also arranges transportation for the family to the funeral and the graveside. He provides a visitor's book for the foyer of the funeral home or church, collects all the cards and notes accompanying the floral tributes, and writes down the names of the flowers in the arrangements. He makes out as many death certificates as he is asked for, and he arranges for collection of burial insurance, veteran's burial compensation, and social security burial benefits. The director also puts the family in contact with the cemetery where the lot is to be purchased. If the burial is to be in a country cemetery, he usually contacts a vault company to see that the grave is prepared. All of this is included in the services paid by the family. It is good to know this, as it will save the family much trouble if they rely upon an establishment that is set up to take care of such matters.

It has been said that the difference between mediocrity and outstanding service is the willingness of a person to do the extra things. If a pastor wants to be an outstanding servant of his people, the prefuneral services offer him a great opportunity. Some of these things he should do because they are nothing more than the thoughtful gesture of genuine neighborliness, to say nothing of Christian concern. One good meal a day, including the day of the funeral, should be served at the home where most of the family is likely to gather. Prior to the funeral, the washing and cleaning of the clothes can be arranged, making certain that clothes needed for the funeral are made ready.

If there is much coming and going from the home of the deceased, there should be a host from the church to greet the visitors and offer them the guest book to sign. The host may need to shield the bereaved from too much company or from some of the company who comes. The host will also assist in serving and try to make all present comfortable in whatever way is possible.

During the funeral, it is good to see that the house is cleaned and aired and changed about some. Coming into a different arrangement may be helpful for the family. The family also appreciates a meal prepared for them in their absence, inasmuch as some will be leaving right away to return to their homes out of town.

Finally, there is the funeral itself. The purpose is to honor the memory of the departed, comfort the bereaved, and undergird the faith of the Christians in a coming resurrection. Each funeral service should be a personal concern of the pastor. There is no excuse for using a cut and dried sermon for every funeral. This event is a shocking, terrifying experience for the family, and a minister is unworthy of his calling unless he takes it as a personal responsibility and makes his address very warm, kind, and personal.

It is not a good idea to have several ministers give sermons. Nor should the service go beyond forty minutes. The usual service arrangement is about the same, but the funeral director, the singers, and the organist should receive a copy of the schedule.

At the conclusion of the service, the pastor stands at the head of the casket, ready to assist the bereaved and to comfort them in any way possible. When the casket is moved to the hearse and then from the hearse to the graveside, he always precedes it. After the committal at the graveside, he should speak again with the family, assure them that he will be praying for them, and ask them to call him in any time of further need.

Should a pastor accept a fee for his service? If the family is a member of his congregation, he definitely should not. This is a part of his pastoral duty. If, however, his service involved some distance of travel, it is suitable for him to accept a gift as a defrayal of his expenses. If the funeral is for a stranger to himself and to the church, the minister can use his own judgment as to whether he accepts a fee or not.

On the second day after the funeral it is proper for the pastor to make a call at the home of the bereaved. He will find the family very glad to see him, as they will want to express their appreciation to him for his great help and understanding. They are sure to be lonely, and his visit will mean more to them than he can realize. He will want to speak good words about the deceased. Through the memory of others they catch a glimpse of their loved one again, and in some ways this is the nearest the bereaved can get to the one who has left them. Kind words concerning the deceased correspond with the tender feeling they have in their heart, and this establishes a mutual fellowship, which is very comforting to those who care so much.

This visit should be cheery. The pastor should point out the blessings that come to them in life, things they have to be thankful for. He should come in with a smile on his face and leave with one, so they will feel that the sun has shone through the clouds again.

One of the last items ending the pastor's responsibility during this time of bereavement is to send a kind letter with a bit of assuring poetry or a comforting passage of Scripture a few weeks after the funeral. Things of this nature are never forgotten, and strangely they seem to arrive in the home of good church members just when they seem to need them the most.

Serving people grandly, graciously, and spiritually is a work of art. It should be the desire of every preacher to excel in this area.

9

The Minister and Authority

The Pentecostal movement has justly laid much stress upon the leading doctrines of the faith. However, it has seemingly relegated the matter of church government to the status of minor consequence. In this chapter, we do not attempt to justify or to discredit current methods, but we will discuss the teaching of the New Testament on the organization and administration of the church. The Bible is clear, both in precept and apostolic example, about the principles of leadership and authority.

The purpose of this chapter is not to justify or encourage ministerial tyranny. Power exercised by humans is ugly at its best; when naked, it is doubly so. But when the lust of power is wrapped in the clothes of the clergy, it is repugnant beyond words. Authority exercised for the good of the church and for righteousness is one thing, but when the motive is purely personal, its selfish purpose is obvious and justly resented. The ministry should never forget the advice that the aged apostle gave the young preacher in II Timothy 2:24-25: "And the servant of the Lord must not strive; but be gentle unto all men, apt to teach, patient, in meekness instructing those that oppose themselves."

There is no scriptural justification for a brute display of raw dictatorial power and spirit in a Pentecostal church. Anyone who will quote from this chapter and not from the following one, is unfair, for the latter shows the other side of the coin. In this chapter, we consider the divine provision of ministerial authority, which we hold to be God's divine plan and intent.

Since people often exercise their will and choice according to their varied backgrounds and temperaments, they seldom reach the absolute ideal in all church procedures. Just as people sometimes fail to exercise the gifts of the Spirit properly and to manifest the fruit of the Spirit fully, so also some churches do not always enact the ideal of New Testament church government.

The wise minister simply takes people as they are and, with love, understanding, and patience, attempts to lead them where they should go. If the transition from one position to another is to be sound it must take place with the consent of their will. The religious leader does not have to be very old to know that in order to change any religious structure, he must first change the people. Cold laws and carnal manipulations never fix problems. They only create more.

Among the many changes that usually take place in a religious movement as it grows older is the change in the position of authority. As the body matures, the swelling lay membership, because of disappointments in leadership or through natural assertiveness, bit by bit demands and secures a greater voice in church government. This trend is not just a general fact but a danger to the strong and positive message that must be declared from Pentecostal pulpits if they are to remain separate and distinct.

Revelation 2-3 contains messages to seven churches of Asia Minor. While they were actual churches in the first century, they represent situations and problems that can occur in every age, and many people also see them as prophetic of seven phases in church history. The last church was Laodicea, which in many ways exhibits the problems of the present church era. John addressed the seven churches as "the church of Ephesus," "the church in Smyrna," "the church in Pergamos," "the church of Thyatira," "the church in Sardis," "the church in Philadelphia," and "the church of the Laodiceans." The last designation is different from the rest. He did not call it a church of Jesus Christ in Laodicea, but the church of the Laodiceans. The implication is that the church in Laodicea was owned and ruled by the people of Laodicea.

The definition of "Laodicea" itself supports this point. Smith's *Bible Dictionary* gives the meaning as "justice of the people." Ironsides interpreted it to mean "rights of the people." Newell said *laos* means "the people" and *dikio* means "to rule," with the resulting definition being "rule of the people." Ironsides commented, "Could any other term set forth the condition of present church affairs? It is the era of democratization, both in the world and in the church. The terrific slogan, 'vox populi vox dei' or 'The voice of the people is the voice of God,' is ringing through the world with clarionlike distinctiveness."

While these voices and opinions clamor through the world, it is both instructive and wise to take the plain example of the New Testament church as a pattern in all things.

The Origin of a Government Determines the Origin of Power

Most governmental organizations come forth either from the mind of God or the mind of humans. In the realm of human government, people choose the type of government they want. In this arrangement, the source of authority rests with the people, since the institution itself was born of their choice. They are its creator and thus have the power to control and modify it at will.

By the same token, a divine government is amenable only to God, its creator. It is to continue in the force and order in which it was originally conceived. It is an ordinance of God and, as such, is not subject to any modifications or changes by humans. That God Himself has decreed it lends it unchangeableness and dignity.

The church is a divine institution and is to be directed by governments holy in their origin. The solemn charge to Moses was: "And look that thou make them after their pattern, which was shewed thee in the mount" (Exodus 25:40). God gave minute and specific instructions for constructing the place of worship and for conducting that worship. Jewish history shows, both by precept and example, that divinity graced this grand institution only so long as its leaders and Israel conformed to the pattern God showed Moses on the mount. If the "shadows of things to come" (Colossians 2:17) was so definite and clear, how much more precise should be the true object, the church, in its order and government?

God provided leaders for the church before there was a church. Before He brought the New Testament church into existence, Christ had already arranged for its leadership. Acts 1:20, 25 discloses that prior to the birth of the church the twelve apostles had a "bishoprick . . . a ministry and apostleship." Mark 3:14 tells that Jesus "ordained" the Twelve. In Matthew 10:40 Jesus told them, "He that receiveth you receiveth me." Thus there emerges, even before the setting up of the New Testament church, an order of jurisdiction. Divine sovereignty does not rise up out of the church body with its permission; God provided a plan of leadership and handed it down from above. Spiritual authority is not a product of the church but a higher order that existed before there was a church. It is jurisdiction delegated from the hand of God. The purpose of spiritual leadership is not to glorify individuals as "lords over God's heritage" but to supply unfettered, responsible care to the church for which Christ gave Himself. (See I Peter 5:3.) God commissioned this ministry to care for the church. It is responsible for the local church but not subject to the local church.

The prerogatives of the apostles increased as the time neared for the setting up of the church. At first the Lord instructed them: "Go not into the way of the Gentiles, and into any city of the Samaritans enter ye not: but go rather to the lost sheep of the house of Israel" (Matthew 10:5-6). So that they would be better prepared to understand and accept the mysteries of the kingdom, He unfolded His plan to them step by step.

In Matthew 28:19-20, the Lord ordered them to "teach all nations." In Mark 16:15, He commanded them to "preach the gospel to every creature." No longer was their labor restricted to the Jews, for His death broke down "middle wall of partition" between Jew and Gentile (Ephesians 2:14). "Then said Jesus to them again, Peace be unto you: as my Father hath sent me, even so send I you. . . . Whose soever sins ye remit, they are remitted unto them; and whose soever sins ye retain, they are retained" (John 20:21, 23). Just as God had sent the man Christ with power and authority to execute God's business on earth, so Christ sent the apostles. To them He gave the authority to remit sins in the physical absence of Jesus, by employing His name in baptism.

Authority in the Church Comes from God

The apostles had all the divine authority they needed to execute their great mission, and they were individually called. Christ still holds to the same procedure of personally calling His leaders or ministers. The United Pentecostal Church International believes that the hand of God should precede the hand of the presbytery in the calling of a minister. Twenty-eight years after Christ chose His first apostles, Paul wrote I Corinthians 12:28: "And God hath set some in the church, first apostles, secondarily prophets, thirdly teachers, after that miracles, then gifts of healings, helps, governments, diversities of tongues." God reserves for Himself the right to call people to certain functions of the church.

As a person's gift makes way for him, the presbytery is duly authorized to ordain him to the ministry unto which God has already called him. The apostles did not have power to delegate their office and authority to others whom they themselves chose as their successors. It is

God who sets people in certain offices, and it is the office itself in which He has vested the needed authority.

Jesus asked in Matthew 23:19, "For whether is greater, the gift, or the altar that sanctifieth the gift?" When someone placed a gift on the altar, it became part of the whole purpose for the altar. Therefore, Jesus continued, "Whoso therefore shall swear by the altar, sweareth by it, and by all things thereon" (Matthew 23:20). Similarly, when someone receives a spiritual office, he receives the sanctification and authority that belongs to the office.

Offices are not necessarily for life, however, for though Judas had been ordained to a ministry, bishopric, and apostleship, he fell from them all. He was not swallowed up in the claims and intent of the altar, nor was he at one with its purpose.

Was spiritual authority resident only in the apostles, or does it rest also upon other leaders whom God calls, even to the end of the church age? In the sense of inspiration to write Scripture, the apostolic age was unique. But the commission to preach to all the world is to continue until the end of the world. Therefore, spiritual leaders must still have the authority to preach, baptize, and carry out other responsibilities that Jesus originally gave to the apostles. In order to be effective, the message must be authoritatively presented by one sent from God.

Sovereignty must rest somewhere in all governments. The extremes of opinion in the church world range from the Roman Catholics, who have one individual as the absolute church head, to independent churches, who often claim that the highest authority in the church rests in each congregation collectively. What does the Bible say?

Nowhere does the New Testament say that jurisdiction resided in local or collective churches. In every instance of decision or administration in the apostolic churches, authority rested in the office of the ministry. It was the ministers who shepherded them and organized the churches. Before there was a New Testament church, there were ordained ministers. From this arrangement, impregnated with God's power, churches came forth.

Paul labeled the Galatian church "my little children, of whom I travail in birth." He wrote to the Corinthians, "It pleased God by the foolishness of preaching to save them that believe." He asked the Romans, "How shall they hear without a preacher?" (See Galatians 4:19; I Corinthians 1:21; Romans 10:14.) In the civil realm, a society has an inherent right to govern itself; but a church can expect divine favor only so long as it practices divine procedure.

Church Government in the Beginning

When we start with the church at its birth on the Day of Pentecost and follow it briefly through its operations, we see the pattern of ministerial authority in every instance. Acts 2 records that three thousand souls were added to the church on the first day. Without proper procedure, such growth in one day would certainly produce disorder. But God had the matter well in hand, with twelve trained men ready to administrate and one to do the preaching on the first day. Jesus did not want His church to be a mob, for He opposed such disorganization.

Since the first day of creation, when God separated light from darkness, part of God's program has been to bring order out of chaos. Israel came out of Egypt as a gigantic mob of slaves, but at the end of forty years of training under God, they were a closely knit, highly organized, marching, militant band of people, more than two million strong. They held their leader, Moses, in such respect that in many ways he spoke and acted "instead of God" (Exodus 4:16). In the New Testament, Jesus made a crowd of five thousand sit in companies upon the ground before He fed them.

God did not give the large church in Jerusalem the right to formulate its own laws or to govern itself. Such power rested in the hands of the ministry. "And they continued stedfastly in the apostles' doctrine and fellowship" (Acts 2:42). Nor did the governmental pattern change when another few thousand were saved. About this time they sold their possessions, and they "brought the prices of the things that were sold, and laid them down at the apostles' feet" (Acts 4:34-35). Even the administrative side of the church, including the treasury, was in the hands of the ministry. This was New Testament procedure.

Some believe that Acts 6:1-6 indicates a relinquishing of authority into the hands of the laity:

"And in those days, when the number of the disciples was multiplied, there arose a murmuring of the Grecians against the Hebrews, because their widows were neglected in the daily ministration. Then the twelve called the multitude of the disciples unto them, and said, It is not reason that we should leave the word of God, and serve tables. Wherefore, brethren, look ye out among you seven men of honest report, full of the Holy Ghost and wisdom, whom we may appoint over this business. But we will give ourselves continually to

171

prayer, and to the ministry of the word. And the say-ing pleased the whole multitude: and they chose Stephen, a man full of faith and of the Holy Ghost, and Philip, and Prochorus, and Nicanor, and Timon, and Parmenas, and Nicolas a proselyte of Antioch: whom they set before the apostles: and when they had prayed, they laid their hands on them."

We should note that none of the congregation pro-posed a solution to the problem. The church had the problem, but its solution came from the ministry. The apostles moved on their own accord, without a request from the congregation. Upon their own volition, they called the multitude to them and instructed them to pro-duce seven men from among themselves, whom the apos-tles could appoint. The apostles themselves determined the qualifications that these seven were to possess. Clearly, they would not have accepted them if they had not met these qualifications. The final choice lay with the ministry.

The ministry saw a need, moved to meet it, proposed a solution, and finally, at its own discretion, executed it. Nowhere is the slightest indication that they gave any part of the power of the ministry to the congregation. At no time, here or elsewhere, did the congregation determine church policy and hand it to the ministry. Always in the New Testament, the ministry determined policy and dele-gated it to and through the church.

A common assumption rising out of this episode is that these seven men were the first deacons in the New Testament church. The inference is drawn since "deacon" in I Timothy 3:10 and "serve" in Acts 6:2 are both translated from the Greek word *diakoneo*, which is the root for the English word *deacon*. Perhaps the men in Acts 6 were deacons, but the Scriptures do not definitely state that they were. They may have been no more than an ad hoc committee, soon dissolved when the need for it passed.

At this point, it is good to notice that Scripture nowhere gives the duties of a deacon, although I Timothy 3:8-13 states their qualifications in detail. Why this apparent oversight? We cannot question the wisdom of the Bible, so undoubtedly there was a good reason for not identifying their duties. Apparently, they were to assist the ministry, and for the sake of flexibility, the Bible leaves their stipulated duties to the discretion of each minister.

God knows that customs and conditions vary with time, region, and culture. Churches might be large or small, rural or urban, English or Japanese, each with its own peculiarity and need. Thus, the role of the deacon varies with the need of each pastor and church. It seems that God has left the pastor to determine the deacon's duties. If he has a duty at all in the church, it must be delegated to him from one higher in authority than he, since the biblical record is silent. This source would be his pastor.

Some believe that deacons were lay preachers in the local church who assisted the elders (ministry). Paul said, "For they that have used the office of a deacon well purchase to themselves a good degree, and great boldness" (I Timothy 3:13). In other words, they graduated into the active ministry of the Word. If the seven men of Acts 6 were indeed deacons, this point would seem to have merit, for at least two of them—Stephen and Philip—did become active ministers of the Word.

In terms of spiritual authority, then, the church is not a corporation with the deacons as the board of directors. Nor are the deacons the supreme policy-making committee or legislative body. However, they could function in this role and more if the pastor appoints them to be, for they are to assist him in whatever he needs.

The Authority of the Apostles and Elders

After the church was thirteen years old, it confronted a major decision, namely, the appropriate church policy relative to circumcision. Several outstanding facts of New Testament church government come to light as we examine the deliberations in this matter, as recorded in Acts 15.

Because of dissension at Antioch, the local church decided to send Paul and Barnabas to Jerusalem to ask the apostles and elders about the matter. It appears that the church at Antioch would have decided the question to its own satisfaction if it had possessed the sovereign right to govern itself independently, but the supreme seat of spiritual and doctrinal authority did not rest in the local church. There was an interchurch responsibility, and the highest spiritual authority was outside the local church. It was to this leadership that Paul and Barnabas appealed for a ruling on the problem.

Elsewhere we see the authority of the spiritual leadership in Jerusalem, regarding both ministers and churches, in that four years earlier, they had called on Peter to account for the visit he paid to Cornelius's house (Acts 11). The same leadership structure operated when they ruled forthrightly and objectively concerning a replacement for Judas (Acts 1). That was their first administrative decision, and they made it even before the

New Testament church came into being. Thirteen years later the spiritual authority of the church still operated as it did in the beginning.

The ruling of the apostles and elders in Jerusalem discloses that they expected the cooperation of all the local churches. James, the presiding elder, gave a summary statement that was nothing less than an authoritative document, obligatory on the churches of Antioch, Syria, and Cilicia. "Wherefore my sentence is," stated the chairman. (See Acts 15:19.) By the virtue of his office, he had the authority to make a summary and pass a sentence that affected churches he had never set foot in. This summary was the opinion reached by the ministerial body in session. They acted in full harmony with God's will, as we see by the preface of their decree: "For it seemed good to the Holy Ghost, and to us" (Acts 15:28).

It is instructive to pay close attention to the procedure of this high-level meeting in Jerusalem. First, Paul and Barnabas declared to all the church body, including the apostles and elders, the working of God among the Gentiles. They spoke at an open church service, attended by all. But because the status of Gentiles in the church was controversial, there was next a closed meeting of the apostles and elders. Once again, we see that in the New Testament church, the laity were not involved in determining church policy; it was formulated by the ministry.

In this closed session the minister debated the question and arrived at a decision, which they sent to all the churches as a ruling of the supreme authority of the church in session. The words of James in verses 24 and 28—"we gave no such command" and "lay upon you no greater burden"—indicate that these leaders had the power both to give commands and to lay burdens. They disclosed their decision to the whole church, and everyone was happy with the solution.

Who Were the Elders?

Not only did the apostles deliberate on this question, but so did the elders. Who were these men? The first reference to elders in the New Testament church is in Acts 11:30, which speaks of them as holding a position of authority in the church at Jerusalem, about nine years after Pentecost. At this time, the church in Jerusalem numbered at least ten thousand people filled with the Holy Ghost. This vast multitude had no building of their own. Before the second persecution they worshiped at Solomon's Porch (Acts 5:12) and in the streets. No doubt, there were many scattered services conducted all through the day, and studies were in progress all over the city.

To lead and guide so great a number there was, of necessity, much leadership. Not even the twelve apostles were sufficient for the job. Thus, in Jerusalem there emerged another group of the ministry, called "elders." No doubt they were some of the 120 who received the Holy Ghost on the Day of Pentecost (Acts 1:15), or at least some of the more than 500 who saw the resurrected Christ (I Corinthians 15:6).

The next reference to elders is in Acts 14:23, where Paul and Barnabas on their return to Jerusalem revisited the churches they had established on their way out from Antioch. There, with prayer and with fasting, they had "ordained them elders in every church." These churches had been in operation for two years. In this lapse of time, and in the process of conducting their own services, divine leadership became apparent within the assembly. By the time Paul and Barnabas got back around to them, it was not hard to see whom God had laid His hand upon in each congregation. Acting upon the authority invested in them as apostles (Acts 14:1-4), they ordained these men as elders in the church. These men were the spiritual leaders, or pastors, of the church.

Why do we find "elders" in the plural? We must remember the conditions in those days, such as the lack of housing and transportation. The mass meetings of the church were probably nothing more than open-air street services. Much of the ministry of the Word took place, as in Jerusalem, from house to house, in cottage prayer meetings, and in countless smaller groups where the closeness of residence erased the travel problem. Imparting the Word took much time, for the meetings were small and numerous and required considerable leg-work. Therefore, each local assembly usually had more than one man who served as elder or pastor. Considering all factors, the likelihood of conflict was almost nil. The fast-expanding assemblies probably gave each elder or pastor more work than he could take care of.

Timothy and Titus received their ordination by the laying on of the hands of Paul and the presbytery. (See I Timothy 4:14; II Timothy 1:6.) They, in turn, used the delegated authority of Paul to ordain elders in the region surrounding Ephesus and on the island of Crete. (See Titus 1:5.) Doing so was not a matter of one person passing along a resident office to a successor. God had already called these people. The presbytery recognized this call by the laying on of hands in ordination. The method of leaving the church after its birth and coming back to establish a pastor in it, seems to be the pattern that Paul followed. To fully appreciate this procedure, we must understand that he was operating in raw mission fields at a time when there was no backlog of preachers to draw from or Bible schools to help in instructing them.

From Titus 1:5-7, we see that the words *elder* (Greek, *presbuteros*) and *bishop* (Greek, *episcopas*) designate the same office. Most students of New Testament church government agree that it is impossible to differentiate the office of elder from that of bishop (overseer). The terms are used interchangeably. To understand clearly an elder's duty, let us read Paul's charge to the Ephesian elders. Every Pentecostal pastor today should endeavor to fulfill these duties. The charge appears in Acts 20:28-31:

"Take heed therefore unto yourselves, and to all the flock, over the which the Holy Ghost hath made you overseers, to feed the church of God, which he hath purchased with his own blood. For I know this, that after my departing shall grievous wolves enter in among you, not sparing the flock. Also of your own selves shall men arise, speaking perverse things, to draw away disciples after them. Therefore watch, and remember, that by the space of three years I ceased not to warn every one night and day with tears."

The elders who participated in the conference of Acts 15 and who were duly ordained in every church, were, in reality, the pastors and ministers of those churches. Today, transportation, printing and the telephone, along with the ability to gather the entire congregation under one roof at each meeting, enables one person to be the pastor of far more people than was possible in the days of the apostles. Moreover, large churches today typically have several ministers providing pastoral care under the leadership of a senior pastor.

Summary of Spiritual Authority in the Church

After the apostles died, who exercised spiritual authority and leadership in the church? The participation of the elders in the conference at Jerusalem in Acts 15 indicates that they were the ones who did so. Spiritual authority rested with those who continued in the ministry that Jesus commissioned the apostles to fulfill, namely, the preaching of the gospel and the remitting of sins through baptism. The supreme authority under God for the New Testament church is the ministerial body of the church in session, as we see in Acts 15.

Primarily, the ministry held supreme authority collectively, as Jesus indicated by giving the great commission to His apostles as a group. The ministry had unique decision-making authority, as we see in Acts 5:1-11; 8:20-23; 14:14-18, and other passages. Under God's direction, Peter made a unilateral decision to preach to the Gentiles, but since this step had important implications for the whole church, he came under collective scrutiny for his actions. (See Acts 10-11.) In matters of general application, which involved all the churches, such as the question of circumcision, decision-making power rested in the collective ministry.

Paul, though the apostle to the Gentiles, with the right to delegate authority both to Timothy and Titus, recognized the authority of the collective body. Like Peter, he submitted to the collective leadership of the elders in Jerusalem. (See Acts 21:17-26.)

We can plainly and easily understand the overall structure of the New Testament church. Its most outstanding factor was the recognition of authority under God that rested in the hands of its ministry. The shepherd's office was one of care and gentle concern. He was not a head-knocker, but a saver of souls.

There are two kinds of churches that will not prosper. One is where the pastor is an iron-fisted dictator, holding the saints in fear. The other is where the pastor is only a figurehead—where the church or certain members of the church set the pastor aside and run the church to suit themselves.

Hebrews 13:7, 17 is an apt closing for this review of New Testament church government:

"Remember them which have the rule over you, who have spoken unto you the word of God: whose faith follow, considering the end of their conversation. . . . Obey them that have the rule over you, and submit yourselves: for they watch for your souls, as they that must give account, that they may do it with joy, and not with grief: for that is unprofitable for you."

10

The Minister and His Relations with His Brethren

Ministerial relations are not quite like those in other spheres of life. The character of the ministry accents the joy of such relations but also makes them more complex. There are not many times or places where the minister can absolutely relax among those who will understand his problems and speak his language. This accounts for the jolly mood in the foyer of the conference auditorium and on the grounds of the district camp. Good-natured banter and brotherly love are sunshine along many a tired preacher's pathway. Perhaps nowhere on earth is there a more sincere and enjoyable relationship than between ministers, when it is at its best.

As both churches and preachers grow in number, however, ministerial society becomes more complex. Some pastors and churches now have neighboring fellowships in the same city with them where ten years ago they labored alone. In situations so intimate there remains the possibility of keen disappointment. The ministerial call does not exclude difficulties of fellowship potent enough to sour the closest relations. This being true, wisdom suggests an ethical code of ministerial conduct whereby fellowship can be established upon the basis of mutual compatibility.

All professions that seek harmonious working relationships have adopted codes of ethics. Lawyers feel that they have a right to disbar any of their profession who might become a detriment to the practice. The medical profession has likewise established certain rules of conduct for its members.

Understanding is the heart of harmony. Hence, in this chapter we consider briefly various areas of responsibility, influence, and rectitude that are pertinent to the ministerial office.

Avoid the Rudeness of Noncooperation

There is a reason why occasionally a preacher withdraws to himself and becomes a lone wolf. Some are so filled with self-love that they have no room to consider community needs. Having certain native abilities of administration and oratory, they are able to build about themselves walls of security behind which they comfortably retire and rebuff any involvement that would not contribute further to their own selfish well-being.

How inclusive is the inspired advice that Paul offered along this line: "Let nothing be done through strife or vainglory; but in lowliness of mind let each esteem other better than themselves. Look not every man on his own things, but every man also on the things of others" (Philippians 2:3-4).

In this world, the common practice is to stand on another's neck in order to reach a little higher. The swift dig of the elbow is standard where a sly inference can be dropped on the side. "But it shall not be so among you" Jesus said (Matthew 20:26). For Christians in general, and certainly for ministers, there must be a better way to live among brethren. Everyone has witnessed strong and capable people who withdraw into the place of their self-content, perhaps doing a good work locally but denying themselves the opportunity of a richer and more widespread ministry among the brethren. The general organization is also cheated of their influence and talents. There is no good work that a noncooperative preacher does that would not be enhanced and blessed further if he were in complete harmony with his brethren.

Much of the work of some ministers has been wasted because they could not labor in accord with the body of believers. Some years ago, a man whose ministry had left its mark across the nation passed away. Immediately the great work he had done at the cost of many thousands of dollars began to disintegrate because he had not tied it to something higher and greater than himself. Life is such a short thing at its best; what right-thinking person would not want capable people to perpetuate the fruits of his labor, doing so in fond memory of a close fellowship they had with him in times past?

Paul's philosophy of the unison and congeniality by which we are to accomplish God's work is worth our consideration. I Corinthians 3:5-10 says:

"Who then is Paul, and who is Apollos, but ministers by whom ye believed, even as the Lord gave to

every man? I have planted, Apollos watered; but God gave the increase. So then neither is he that planteth any thing, neither he that watereth; but God that giveth the increase. Now he that planteth and he that watereth are one: and every man shall receive his own reward according to his own labour. For we are labourers together with God: ye are God's husbandry, ye are God's building. According to the grace of God which is given unto me, as a wise masterbuilder, I have laid the foundation, and another buildeth thereon. But let every man take heed how he buildeth thereupon."

Paul went ahead to describe the materials a person could use in building on this million-dollar foundation. He cautioned, however, that everyone's work would be tried by fire. The work of many noncooperative preachers has not stood the test of time, so how could such efforts bear the scrutiny of eternity?

Not only does selfishness prompt a person to non-conformity with a healthy fellowship, but fear does so as well. Some people are too small to stand alone, and others are so small they fear not to stand alone. They are afraid of being trampled. Their approaches, behavior, and pet ideas sometimes will not bear exposure to close fellowship and intimate examination, so they retreat to a personal jurisdiction where, without fear of being stepped on, they can yelp loudly and safely.

It is much better to sit down with brethren and talk, rather than to backbite and pull away. If, because of scruples, a person cannot endorse a certain project or program, he can usually state his position in such a way, and with the kind of spirit, that leaves all parties concerned still loving one another. Always the nonconformist should examine himself to be sure he has not adopted his stance merely for selfishness or expediency's sake. To be honest, we should admit that the fellowship has quite an investment in most preachers and thus is not beyond the bounds of reason to expect their cooperation wherever they can conscientiously give it.

Sometimes it is not to the good of the local church program to cooperate in a particular endeavor. Local revivals, for example, sometimes make a difference. Church loyalty is a necessary and precious thing in a local assembly. Churches, like families, cannot maintain their discipline and allegiance to themselves unless in some things they remain distinct. This is understandable and allowable.

Shun the Smallness of Intolerance

God in His wisdom has endowed His preachers with a variety of ministries. The emphasis in each person's preaching varies tremendously, even though most hold the same truths. Differences in background, home life, and personal temperaments contribute a great deal to the variety that exists in the United Pentecostal Church fellowship. This trait is not peculiar to our day, but it was found among the first apostles, as a casual look will reveal. They all believed the same thing, but they differed in their emphasis. A comparison of Galatians and James will substantiate this statement. Happily, in the framework of organization, we have agreed upon the Articles of Faith, set forth in the Manual of the United Pentecostal Church International, as expressions of biblical truth and as the basis of our fellowship. To them every United Pentecostal minister should subscribe.

Paul found it necessary to teach on tolerance in Romans 14, relative to the eating of meat. When we apply the law of love to nonmoral questions such as this, we see that tolerance is not a one-way street. Both the abstainers and the participants are to be their brother's keeper; the abstainer is not to judge his brother, and the participant is not to cause his brother to stumble.

In the name of holiness and love for truth, people can say many hard and harmful things. Under the banner of broadmindedness and higher understanding, others can hurl countercharges. Both can be avoided if each proponent will show the other the rightful tolerance on questions that are not distinctly outlined by the accepted basis of the fellowship, while at the same time granting that each has a right, on the same basis, to personal conscientious scruples. Because some preachers are not big enough and patient enough to sit down together and discuss their differences, dissension sometimes prevails. No point of conviction is worth holding if it is not strong enough to bear the scrutiny of personal, friendly discussion. It is cowardly to hide behind the pulpit to deliver arguments and afterward avoid the company of a brother who might not have agreed. Anyone who is unsure of his position probably needs to reevaluate it. Perhaps he does not care enough to be friendly. Regardless of differences between ministers, whether real or imagined, they, as gentlemen, owe to each other the congenial hand of honest friendship.

Instead of such consideration, however, a brother who might differ in practice or technicalities may be criticized—and that to his back. Criticism presents a temptation all its own. There are several reasons for criticism. The criticizer projects himself, either subconsciously or in actuality, as an authority on the point under discussion. To be thus exalted, even though it is of self, is quite an uplift to one's ego. For as long as he talks and people listen, he basks in the warmth of his fancied authoritative position. No wonder the temptation is not only to criticize, but, once started, the temptation is to criticize much, exploring glibly other possible deficiencies of character or intent. Not only does this give the ego a chance to expand, but the criticizer has a chance to supposedly build himself up by tearing down the other preacher. Of course, this method of building does not really work, either on a house or another minister, but intolerance leads the criticizer to practice it anyway.

We could write a book on what motivates preachers to criticize and still not exhaust the subject. Not much space is required, however, to simply state the undeniable fact that criticism always gets back to the one who is talked about. "Where no wood is, there the fire goeth out: so where there is no talebearer, the strife ceaseth" (Proverbs 26:20). Unfortunately, there always seems to be a talebearer, and he will carry to the criticized person the words that can never be taken back.

Without making any effort to understand one another's position and without any personal discussion, some preachers simply, by private and public statements, alienate a brother who could have been a warm and helpful friend to them. Surely brotherly love and personal friendship are more valuable than that! We must be intolerant of sin and false doctrine, but when the basis of a difference is personal opinion or a personality quirk, then intolerance becomes a cruel and needless divider of the brethren.

Certainly a preacher should never criticize other ministers to laity. If he, for conscience' sake, cannot be tolerant of a certain situation, there are other ways for him to handle the problem than by making a frontal attack. In the first place, it is not the right of laity to judge a minister, so why present him for their inspection?

The United Pentecostal Church International has provided a seat of judgment, if such is needed, where preachers manage their own affairs in the proper manner. But when one minister criticizes another before laity, then respect for the ministry, nurtured and cultivated for years in the heart of saints, can be destroyed. And once it is destroyed, it is seldom completely restored. We can in no way justify attacks made from the pulpit on the organization or on other preachers. Why present a problem to a group of laypersons when they are powerless to do anything about it? Such a procedure sows fear, anxiety, and distrust in a helpless flock. It is folly!

A discerning layperson could well make this deduction while listening to such a tirade: "What do you expect me to do about this? Inasmuch as this is preachers' business, I must assume that you have not been taking care of it, or else things wouldn't be in the mess you say they are." It should not be hard for a preacher, even with little discernment, to see that an open attack on another minister destroys in the heart of the layperson the very thing he must depend on for survival—respect for the ministry. How foolish to pull the house down about his own ears!

Fear the Blight of Jealousy

For the most part, preachers live very clean, moral lives, hence meriting for themselves a preferred risk status for several forms of insurance. Though in the eyes of the world the sin question stops with outward behavior and habits, the Spirit searches the heart of the preacher and sometimes uncovers gross and repulsive sins of the spirit. Sin is lawlessness in any form, and though it may for a while be covered by an exterior pretence, in time it will reveal itself.

Jealousy is one of the most prevalent and besetting sins of the ministry. In a fellowship comprising varied strata of income and recognition, it is easy for ministers to compare themselves with each other. Most often, jealousy is a product of inordinate self-love. Its evil presence is felt when others are exalted in offices, congratulations, or preference. It shows itself in relations with a brother and in the appraisal of a brother.

Often, if a certain minister supersedes others by overwhelming acclaim, they are content to wait in his shadow because he, by all evidence, is far above the ordinary and thus out of range of competition. But when a minister sees someone whom he has consciously or subconsciously appraised as being his equal or less, receive the seat above him, at once the green-eyed monster stirs himself. The reason is that the minister has labored closely enough with the successful person to make a comparison feasible, both by himself and others. Somehow he feels that the other's progress accents his failure. How sad it is that some preachers are not only sorrowful over the disappointment that comes to themselves but also over the good that comes to their brothers!

Jealousy burns like fire. (See Psalm 79:5.) The wise man stated, "Jealousy is the rage of a man," and, "Jealousy is cruel as the grave" (Proverbs 6:34; Song of

Solomon 8:6). Experience has proven that jealousy is all the Bible says it is and more. As Saul eyed David with rancor and bitterness, so have other good men come under cold stares as they took their place on the conference rostrum, in a committee, or behind a camp-meeting pulpit.

It seems strange that a preacher should feel resentful toward a brother who is successful in getting done some of the work that hangs heavy upon the shoulders of all. The truth is that the jealous preacher has lost the point and purpose of God's work. Self has usurped the throne of his heart, displacing Christ and the good of God's work in general. He has become discontent against God, yet how can the vessel that is formed say to the potter, "What doest thou?" (See Job 9:12; Daniel 4:35.)

He has forgotten God's authority and the fact that God has the right to set up one and put down another. He has forsaken the teaching of God's Word, which tells us that in honor each is to prefer the other. He becomes blind to the good in the life of his brother, thereby often turning to criticism and sometimes to defamation.

In time, unless the minister removes this evil from his life and heart, he is sure to become bitter, filled with self-pity, unkind, and unapproachable. Needless to say, his fellowship pales and wanes away, lacking the exuberance of a pure heart and the encouragement of an unselfish hand. His sermons lose their punch and prophetic luster, for a corrupt tree cannot bring forth good fruit (Luke 6:43).

Jealousy is sometimes at work in organizational elections when one person, by the decision of the brethren, is asked to step down in favor of another. A district official made a true statement some years ago when he said, "You will know exactly what kind of man I am when I am voted out of this office."

Some pastoral successors find it hard not to be jealous of the person they have succeeded. The comparisons that the congregation naturally makes always seem to place the new pastor in the position of competing with his predecessor for their love and respect. If he allows it, he can, with the help of the devil, create a ghost of the former pastor to haunt him, dog his footsteps throughout the day, and taunt him in every major decision. How much better it is simply to refuse to compete; to concede, early and continually, that the former pastor is tops in all things; and to state that the wonderful thing is that he is privileged to be the former pastor's friend!

Jealousy is one of the greatest poisons of the ministry. Most preachers are not novices in the workings of the spirit world and should be discreet enough to dash jealousy's cup from their lips without even tasting. If a fellow minister is on his way up, how much better it is to deposit in him an investment of sincere prayer and friendship that will later come back in dividends rich and numerous, than to enter spiritual suit against him and receive back the bitter fruit of what was sown! At any rate, how foolish it is to fight against God!

The Relationship of a Host Pastor to a Visiting Minister

As we have already stated, the preacher should, of all things, be a gentleman. As such, he will endeavor to be congenial and gracious as a host to the minister who visits his home or church. Public speaking, along with painting and drama, is classed among the fine arts. The host pastor should excel in the fine art of sociality. Great feasts and entertainment are not necessary. The simple, deft act of putting people at ease, and showing that they are wanted and appreciated, can be initiated in many telling and personal ways.

V. A. Guidroz often recounted how this trait seemed to be so grandly perfected by the late W. T. Witherspoon. Brother Witherspoon would not allow a visiting minister to park his automobile outside the garage but insisted on parking his own outside so that his visitor might use the garage for his car. He was careful to help his visitor with his luggage and try to make sure all of his needs were taken care of before he left him. Many a visiting preacher would awake to find the morning paper under his door. The kind thoughtfulness of this great man made a lasting impression on all who were privileged to stay in his home.

There is a distinct art to being a good host. Courtesy and Christian kindness should, in themselves, be sufficient motives to encourage one to really try in this field. Inasmuch as the visiting minister is both a brother and a guest, attention and consideration for his comfort should be given ungrudgingly.

The visiting minister, of course, should have a comfortable place to stay. If he is to stay in the parsonage, it is best if the guest room is near the bath and so situated that an early riser would not disturb others. Moreover, the host should not begrudge extra sleep in the morning or rest in the afternoon for a hard-working evangelist who lavishly spends his strength and energy in sermon and altar work each night.

If the church is fortunate enough to have evangelistic quarters, the evangelist is likely to enjoy his stay all the more. While a single man might prefer staying with the pastor and his family in the parsonage, most married couples, especially if they have children, prefer to stay in the evangelistic quarters.

Even with a single minister, a certain strain is thrown on the parsonage by having a visitor in the home, though the friendship be ever so warm. To be responsible for the comfort and welfare of a visitor and at the same time carry a burden for souls, is taxing in the course of a long series of meetings. The pastor should at this time be visiting with people and pushing the evangelistic program relentlessly. In the heat of such endeavors, instruction to seekers and to new converts can require more time in counseling than he would ordinarily expend. The pastor thus is burdened enough with the added pastoral responsibility engendered by the revival, without adding an entertainment schedule.

Perhaps the pastor's wife carries by far the greater load of entertainment when the evangelist stays with the pastor. Most good women are anxious to please and thus feel obligated to prepare extra dishes and take extra care about the general housework. All the while, the ordinary chores of the church continue and are multiplied because of the extra revival effort.

If she has children of school age, which is more than likely, her rising time remains the same as always, with little hope for extra rest during the day. At night after the service, she must not only hurry the children off to bed but perhaps prepare food or refreshment for her visitors. When this situation is protracted considerably, the result is likely to be a tired, nervous, frustrated pastor's wife.

For these and many more reasons, it is better for the

church to provide ample quarters for the evangelist. Of course, these quarters should have as many comforts and conveniences as one would expect in a modern furnished apartment or motel room. Certainly the room should be clean and supplied with towels and linens. Either the pastor should give to the evangelist an ample grocery check each week, separate from his regular offering, or the pastor should arrange for the delivery of sufficient groceries. At no time should the visitor have to buy with his money food, soap, or other articles that the host would customarily furnish him if he were a guest in the home.

Some churches, having no apartment of their own for the evangelist, will rent one for the duration of the revival. While in some ways this might seem extravagant, considering all things it is certainly justifiable.

The last place that a pastor should place his evangelist is in the home of a church member. The evangelist feels obligated to adapt himself to his host's routine. The early rising, the schedule of meals, acting forever the part of the preacher, and the strain of being among absolute strangers all produce an awkward situation. It is here that the evangelist is in danger of having to listen to problems beyond his jurisdiction to handle, but which the host will probably confide to him if the host comes to love and trust his visitor. Under such circumstances, ethical situations have more than once evolved that have been long-lasting in their embarrassments. If both husband and wife work, the arrangement is perhaps more compatible but still not perfect.

The visiting preacher should also be considerate of his host. If he stays in the pastor's home, he should appreciate the extra strain that his presence brings. While not appearing ill at ease himself, he should strive to make himself as little trouble as possible. If the evangelist's wife is with him, she should not only keep their room but give aid in the general housework as well. Help given with the washing of clothes, cooking, and the washing of dishes will never be forgotten by the tired pastor's wife. Any amount of help would not compensate for the extra strain and workload brought about, both by the revival and the evangelist's presence in the home.

If the evangelist is alone in the revival during his stay at the parsonage, he should certainly keep his own room clean. The pastor's wife should not have to sweep it or make the bed. He should encourage the pastor to feel free to go about the usual tasks of pastoral work. The considerate evangelist knows that all of God's ministers should be busy, and he does not feel slighted if he is left to himself quite a bit during the day. In fact, the man of God who loves study and meditation will generally shun entertainment and would rather that the pastor did not try to arrange his daily schedule for him.

Though the traveling evangelist might preach the same sermons over and over in different churches, the hungry preacher feels his need to broaden himself in other phases of study. Besides this, no one can preach and carry a burden for souls as he should unless he is a man of prayer.

Thus, the evangelist should have enough to do throughout each day so that the busy pastor has no need to turn from his work to entertain him every day. It is good for both evangelist and pastor, along with their wives, to have time for relaxing together on the day of their rest night. Maturity and judgment recognize that on other days the business at hand demands their time and strength. In most enterprises, work and play are not mixed advantageously, and God's work is no exception.

The evangelist is usually willing to make calls with the pastor to the homes of people who may almost be persuaded to make their surrender to God and to the homes of others who may need counsel relative to receiving the Holy Ghost. The discerning pastor, of course, will not call on the evangelist for his company at all times, inasmuch as he wants his visiting preacher at his best every night.

The successful evangelist comes as a friend to both pastor and church. He knows that the welfare of the church is enhanced when the ties that bind pastor and people together are strong. While he is a guest there, he uses the various opportunities that fall into his hands to strengthen those ties even more.

In a few weeks the evangelist will be on his way, and whatever effort he might make to attach people to himself would be both pointless and wasteful. His work in the assembly is but for a short season, but the relationships and the work of the pastor extend through the years. It is better that whatever influence the evangelist might have projected into the assembly be used to solidify and promote the long-term relationship of pastor and people.

At no time should the evangelist hand out advice to the members of the local church unless it be in the presence of the pastor or in close coordination with him. Other professionals who deal with people are careful to confer closely with one another in their prescriptions. In leadership, the voice of authority should not conflict, but the trumpet sound should be sure and certain.

Most of the time when an evangelist finds himself in a

church embroiled in a clash between pastor and church, it is best for him to adopt the blind-eye-and-deaf-ear approach. If the trouble at hand is of long duration, or bitter enough to be open and brash, there is little if any good that the average evangelist can do to fix it. At times there are specially gifted preachers, greatly used of God, who have been instrumental in bringing about equilibrium to a staggering congregation, but this is no ordinary undertaking. Troubles that run deep and have been many years in accumulating and coming to a head, are not dissipated easily by an evangelist with a few sermons. After the barrage from the pulpit has subsided, most likely the bunkers of grudges and hates will still be standing.

About all the average evangelist can do in troublesome situations such as we have described is to pray much himself and do everything he can to get others to pray and worship, so that their eyes might be turned upon Jesus, who teaches everyone to love and to forgive. If he allows himself to become part of the problem, he has disqualified himself to mediate either with God or people.

It is somewhat surprising to know that preachers are not always right. There are times when an evangelist, for conscience' sake, might not be able to support the pastor, either privately or publicly. It is here that the evangelist reaches an ethical impasse. In this case, the best thing for him to do is simply nothing relative to the local problem.

An evangelist does not come to judge such matters, but to speak in a series of meetings that it is hoped will culminate in a revival. If conditions are impossible for revival, he cannot be responsible for conditions beyond his control. He is not empowered to dismiss the pastor, so if prayer and friendly counsel do not help, there is nothing left for the average evangelist to do but gracefully bid everyone adieu at the proper time. If he has come to them night after night with tears, anointing and sincerity, then he has cultivated an atmosphere more conducive to settling the local problem.

In the final analysis, it is the parties involved who must come to Christian terms and fellowship. It is not out of order during a special move of God for the evangelist to open the door for such a reconciliation, but such efforts are liable to do more harm than good unless they are directed strongly by God. Let the evangelist be wise enough to recognize humanly impossible situations and to refrain from being used by an erring pastor instead of God. As we have already pointed out, the evangelist can leave behind a blessing, even if he could not solve the problems.

Since the church supports the evangelist with money, trust, and presence for the duration of a revival, he is obligated to do what he can to strengthen its local program. Some evangelists have been helpful in increasing Sunday school attendance, so that while not many souls may have received the Holy Ghost, new people were introduced to the church through the Sunday school and the church was generally uplifted. Others have imparted a new vision of personal work and soulwinning to the local visitation program. When the visiting minister takes personal interest in bettering the host church, the effort redounds to his own enrichment, both in a spiritual sense and also in the cultivation of friendships across the fellowship.

Besides the salvation of the lost, the foremost goal that the evangelist should have in mind is to deepen the consecration of the church membership. He cannot do so if he has diverted much of his effort to selling himself. God should come first in his projection, pastor and church second, and himself last (or not at all).

The passing years show that when we give Jesus Christ His rightful place of centrality, all other relationships immediately adjust themselves. Any bringing together of people through personal persuasion and talent is only temporary in duration and nil in its effect. The serious minister does not want to thus waste his time building fronts on sinking sand.

Humans must unite with something stronger than themselves if they are to retain integrity through the years. For that reason the evangelist should be careful not to preach himself, but to preach Christ and Him crucified.

During a revival, it is proper for the evangelist to make sincere references to the offerings given by the church and to the kindness shown him by the pastor. He does not have to do so every night, but certainly he should extend warm thanks. After his departure, it is fitting for him to mail a note of remembrance and thanks to the host, who perhaps has gone out of his way to cause the evangelist and his family to have an enjoyable stay.

The Relationship of a Successor
to a Predecessor

Perhaps one of the greatest areas of stress in ministerial fellowship is in the relationship of a successor to a predecessor. Serious problems have evolved when the departing pastor did not have the courage to really say goodbye and the arriving pastor was not big enough to exercise tact through the months of psychological transference of love and leadership recognition. Here are a few helpful points to assure a more graceful exit of a pastor and entrance of his successor.

The pastor who follows another whose pastorate has been successful and of some duration should not be at all surprised that the people still have a strong love in their hearts for the former pastor. At times they will openly declare their love for him, even in a forward and resentful manner. It is not unusual for someone to tell the new pastor quite frankly that no one could ever take the place of their former pastor. Some will extol the former pastor as the greatest in wisdom, patience, and sermonic capability.

At this point, the new arrival can properly comfort himself with an old adage, "Absence makes the heart grow fonder." Experience reveals that a person's best qualities are often appreciated only after his departure. Someday when the new arrival leaves, it will be his turn for the people he has left behind to pledge their love and allegiance to him.

Through the weeks that the new pastor is getting his feet on the ground, he must guard himself against resentment forming in his heart because of the many nice things said about the former pastor. Even when laypersons attempt to be tactful—for example, by adding, "But, of course, we love our present pastor, too," after declaring their love to the former pastor—when they make comparisons, it does not take profound insight for the newcomer to see that they have weighed him in the balance and found him wanting. He should brace himself, as these occurrences will be common for some time if the former pastor was both successful and a long time in residence. Such statements do not imply that the new pastor is not liked; he is simply not liked as well as the former.

It would be quite unfair to human nature to expect all people to love, respect, and appreciate a new pastor as much as they do someone who was with them through the years in all their needs—marital, spiritual, and natural. The successor is wise if he can sympathize with their feeling of loss and love. Such respect for a former pastor should assure him that in time he too, if worthy, will receive the same.

It is almost superfluous to say that the present pastor should not shrink from complimenting his predecessor. Such expression need not be insincere, since everyone should appreciate the good that any minister does in the kingdom of God. The hard work and foresight of the preceding pastor deserve rightful recognition, and to withhold this recognition would not only be unfair but would also reveal the envy and selfishness that fostered such neglect. A capable pastor does not have to be uneasy. He can have assurance that, in time, he will earn his own place and standing as the leader of the congregation.

In time, a confident pastor will not be afraid to ask the former pastor to preach for him. This usually pleases the congregation if the erstwhile pastor had their love and respect. Something about this kind hand of fellowship spreads a mutual confidence throughout the congregation. It erases a talking point from the gossiper's list and clears away a bothersome question that might have been in the minds of others. In addition, the former pastor has a good opportunity to strengthen his successor's hand and solidify support behind the local church, inasmuch as some people are strangely more fond of him after he has gone than when he lived among them as a shepherd.

Blessed is the successor of a pastor whose exit was

wise and graceful enough to encourage such trust and fellowship. Often, the successor will wonder about some things that might occur between the former pastor and his erstwhile charges, but most of these are merely occurrences that are typical in a pastoral transfer.

Sometimes the new pastor may have to turn his head away from a questionable contact by the former pastor and continue to act in good faith toward him. In many cases, unwise actions by both parties have precipitated strife and ill will that darkened the fellowship of capable ministers for many years.

If, after a lapse of time, it becomes clear that the former pastor, for some reason unknown, insists on being a meddler and continues to project his influence into a field that is no longer under his jurisdiction, then the successor can forthrightly take steps to correct the situation. Gentlemen can always afford to be frank and honest with one another. A kind, firm, personal approach to a former pastor's indiscreet behavior is always more profitable than spreading the news with the intent of destroying his influence. Most of the time, if brethren talk kindly enough and long enough, they can reach an understanding.

If the former pastor is in organizational fellowship, it is foolish for a pastor to object to his coming back to his old charge to conduct funerals and weddings. Love and respect, built up sometimes under the most trying circumstances, cannot be turned on and off in the heart of laypersons like water. It is proper for the pastor to help people feel at ease in making a request for their former pastor's participation. Subterfuge and pretext do not cause people to love the new pastor any better. Love grows out of the soil of trust and is most productive in the climate of absolute honesty. The pastor should accept that his people may want their former pastor to officiate and be sensible enough not to argue with reality.

Out of respect and in the light of good judgment, an incoming pastor should give consideration to the outgoing pastor's plans and unfinished programs. Since he had more experience in this particular church and devoted more time to planning his program, to consider it is all the more reasonable.

Usually a new pastor needs all the support of the people as soon as he can get it. He does not ordinarily gain that support by sweeping changes in the church program, unless the whole structure has fallen into decay and the congregation has despaired of it. Some new pastors reappoint all officers immediately, while others choose to wait a year, with the understanding that changes might be forthcoming at that time. The wisdom of change is doubtful unless the change is clearly something better in the eyes of the people. Considering the dislike that people have for the disruption of program and routine, caution should be the first consideration. The new pastor may not have created the circumstances, but he must bear the responsibility of any changes, so they had better be good.

Every Christian appreciates humility. It puts people at ease concerning the minister; they feel they can take him at face value, inasmuch as he will probably not try to sell himself. The mature preacher knows that spiritual growth is usually the result of years of patient toil. Most people reap where others have sown. The newcomer knows that he must lean upon the goodwill and trust of his congregation and depend upon the work of former pastors. The evolution of his status gives no encouragement for him to immediately sound off about his abilities. If he does, the congregation might detect the uncertain note of selfish ego needing assurance. For a while, curiosity will prompt a congregation to listen to a new minister until he can prove himself. But if he creates an image of himself relative to character and abilities that is not true, he simply digs a pit into which he is bound to fall. We cannot emphasize too strongly that honesty is an absolute must in the work of God.

The Relationship of a Predecessor to a Successor

God's minister must remember that he is not his own. Not only was he purchased by the blood of Jesus Christ, but he was also called to a high and holy work. Thus, by virtue of Calvary and the claims of the ministry, he must continually resign himself from selfishness. Nowhere does the edge of a preacher's calling press down more sharply than when God steps into his life and tells him it is time for him to move. Some things about the ministry almost seem cruel in their heartlessness. Divorcing one's heart and presence from a work of years is such an instance. It is here that the leaving pastor must remind himself that the people of the church were not his after all, that they were bought by Christ's blood and belong only to Him.

In a transitional period such as this, the pastor more starkly sees his mission on earth. It is merely to point people to Jesus Christ while he remains in the background. He must accept that whatever good was done in his tenure as pastor, he must not take the credit, since it was God who gave the increase.

It is well for the resigning pastor to explain several things to the church with his resignation. He should make clear the proper organizational procedure to follow until they secure a new pastor. He should assure them that the sectional presbyter and district superintendent are their friends, and admonish the church to work closely with these leaders. Many pastors who have influenced and managed their replacements have later regretted that they did not encourage the church to go through organizational procedures in securing a pastor. They found that though they had left the church they had not left its troubles. Inasmuch as they assumed the responsibility of securing them a pastor, they found themselves also responsible for the outcome.

It is hard for the exiting pastor to cut former ties unless he does so through the mediation of organizational authority that, during the short space of pastoral election, steps between successor and predecessor, giving credence to the severance of one and the installation of the other.

The resigning pastor will save himself and others embarrassment by explaining to the congregation the matters of ministerial ethics and that, while he will always love them, he is no longer their pastor. Such being the case, it would be improper for them to seek his advice hereafter, but they owe this trust to their next pastor. Not only does such an explanation encourage them to seek their counsel at the right seat of authority, but at the same time it may spare the resigning minister the load of continued troubles and problems that he should leave at his old residence.

If the departing pastor is assuming a charge many

miles away from his former church, the likelihood of being tempted to visit his former saints is lessened. After he has transferred pastoral responsibility to another minister's shoulders, it is easy for the former pastor to look upon the people as his warm and intimate friends. He does not have to assume the role of their leader, so he can now let his guard down and just simply be friends.

Most often, the safest thing to do is never to visit in the homes of former saints. The sooner they can transfer pastoral allegiance to the new pastor, the better it is for him and the church as well. If the former pastor projects himself back into his former field by personal visits in the homes of members, the new pastor will not receive the full support that he deserves.

If it is absolutely necessary for a minister to visit in the home of a former saint, it is only fair for him to drop by the parsonage first and bring the new pastor along with him. This thoughtful act demonstrates, as no words could, that the former pastor respects their new leader's position even above the intimacy of his friendship with the saints. This good example will not be lost on them but will encourage them to also grant the new pastor due respect. The least that a visiting predecessor can do is to call the present pastor to tell him what his intentions are. This open, forthright action allays the painful fears and sharp jealousies that often beset a new pastor in a new and strange field.

An evangelist and his wife once made friends with a wonderful couple in a Pentecostal church. The relations were such that they played and picnicked together. Sometimes the pastor, while driving by his saints' home, would be surprised to see the evangelist's car in their driveway. Perhaps he had already spent a night or two under their roof without the pastor's knowing it. Such a situation being very delicate, the pastor was at a loss to know how to adjust the situation tactfully without someone's getting hurt.

As it turned out, the fine Christian laypersons were hurt anyway by the unscrupulous evangelist, who was only playing them for suckers. Their estimation of the ministry as a whole suffered a blow. It is quite hard for any preacher to continually have close fellowship with lay members on grounds of mutuality without causing disappointments and reevaluations.

Any right-thinking person knows that a former pastor will receive invitations to come back to perform weddings and conduct funerals. This is to be expected, especially if his pastorate was of long duration. Such occurrences usually do not unduly alarm the present pastor if the former pastor accepts such invitations discreetly and in good faith. A safe rule to follow is not to accept any invitation unless the person making the invitation has the consent of his present pastor. To be on the safe side, it is best not to simply take the word of the layperson, but to call the pastor personally.

The best procedure is for the former pastor to kindly explain that it is proper for the present pastor to take care of such arrangements and that he is sure that the present pastor would be more than glad to do so. If they would like for him to have a place in the arrangements, they could suggest it and they would probably not be disappointed. He should then assure them that he is willing to work with the pastor in any way.

When a former pastor comes back for any religious

activity, he should never take full charge but only allow for himself the role of assistant to the present pastor. It is good to remember that he is coming into another person's ministerial jurisdiction in which he now has no part. Whatever relations he has carried over from the former association, they should not now go beyond that of friendship.

Here are some steps that the outgoing pastor can take in the transference of pastorates, steps that make for a more smooth and graceful changeover.

First, it is good for the outgoing pastor to discuss the local church organization with the incoming pastor. He should explain the operations of the various departments, along with their relative strengths and weaknesses. He should give his successor a broad outline of his perspective of the work, giving reasons for his conclusions or changes of opinions. He should point out the opportunities of the local church, along with the obstacles.

There are differences of opinion as to whether he should discuss all the church's troubles, some believing that honest ignorance would cause the new pastor to work with fewer inhibitions. On the other hand, who doubts that there are some pitfalls that could prove well nigh fatal to a new pastor, over which ignorance could build no bridge?

If the leaving of one pastor and the coming of another is close enough so that the retiring minister can make a good introduction of the arriving one to the congregation, all the better.

Certainly the departing pastor should clear away all church debts that he possibly can before he leaves town. He should contact the remaining creditors and assure them of the church's intention to pay them. In good faith, some preachers have informed the local church board about the remaining debts. It is much better for them to hear about this from their former pastor than for someone to tell about them after he has gone.

It is important to bring all church records up to date and get them in good shape before a pastor resigns. This includes minutes, financial records, and the membership roll.

The resigning pastor should fully clean the parsonage. He should make a strong effort to gather all belongings so that he will not need to come back.

When a pastor leaves, he should stay gone as much as possible. He has made his decision. He is no longer the pastor of that local church. He cannot have everything in life, so he might as well relinquish his hold upon that church and turn his face and force in the direction of another.

Relationship with Neighboring Pastors

The wise man said that if one is to have friends, he must show himself friendly (Proverbs 18:24). The pastor who imagines that even half of the responsibility of fellowship lies with his neighbor is likely to experience an association that is not exactly ideal. Real fellowships are not composed of people who meet each other halfway.

Fellowship means more than simply doing one's duty. It requires that a person at times go the second mile. Usually, healthy fellowship lies outside the perimeter of the first mile. It is a grand overlapping of mutual respect and willingness to sacrifice to secure and keep the goodwill of a brother.

Neighboring pastors cannot have fellowship unless

both really want it. The considerate preacher is mindful of his brother's feelings when a saint from his brother's church approaches him about changing membership. He senses the disappointment of his brother, and his heart searches as to why such a saint did not choose to remain under his present pastorate. The spiritual pastor remembers that when a saint leaves a church, it causes questions, either spoken or unspoken, among the members. If these kind considerations exist in an area of two or more churches, the chances for compatibility are enhanced.

One Pentecostal minister gave as his reason for being careful in receiving saints from another's church: "I believe that you are bound to reap what you sow." One thing is certain, no fellowship can be established or perpetuated except on the basis of honesty and respect.

Once a pastor becomes convinced that he cannot trust a neighboring pastor, he finds it impossible to receive him wholeheartedly. Thus, each neighboring minister must, for the sake of goodwill, studiously avoid circumstances that in any way would cast doubt on the good faith of his actions.

In making hospital calls, no pastor should visit people who attend another Pentecostal church in the area. They are simply not his business. If, by accident, a good pastor does visit such a room, he should make his visit extremely short, praise their pastor lavishly, and hastily excuse himself.

If, for any reason, a pastor should find it necessary to contact another pastor's member, either by phone or personal visit, it is good to first secure that pastor's permission to do so. This will show his neighbor that his motives are right and in good faith.

There may come a time when a neighboring pastor is away and an emergency arises, necessitating another pastor's stepping in to meet the need. In this case, the pastor should freely give his assistance until the saint's own pastor can be contacted and brought upon the scene; then the minister friend is glad to retire from the scene.

A preacher should be courteous to all, but to be overly solicitous for members of another church is to invite embarrassment. It is said that if you pat a puppy on the head, he will follow you home. Many times the "sheep stealer" talks other minister's members into his fold without ever actually asking them to become a member of his church. But preachers are not blind, and they soon recognize such tactics. One wonders if what the "sheep stealer" gains by such a procedure equals the loss of respect and love that he might ordinarily have among his ministering brethren, not to speak of the loss of God's favor.

11

The Preacher and Harmonious Church Relations

God uses leaders. He has always worked His program through people. In the Old Testament, the patriarchs, priests, and prophets gave strong and positive leadership based on divine intent. Jesus is a great example of the wise use of secondary leadership. The men whom He trained became the foundation stones upon which the church is built. Ephesians 4 states that God has given the fivefold ministry to the church to accomplish His purposes. God did not leave His church without recognized and sufficient leadership.

While this leadership is divinely provided, it rules by the permission of those who are governed by it. The General Conference of the United Pentecostal Church International has determined this to be the best policy and has adopted a system of local church government. Under such an arrangement, the minister belongs to that class of employees who are in a way over their employers, such as the doctor, the lawyer, and the business executive. Under such circumstances, the doctor dictates, the lawyer instructs, and the executive spends the stockholder's money as he thinks best. Yet each of them may have his service terminated by those who have employed him. In like manner, the mayor of a city exercises authority over the citizens who chose him and pay him. These arrangements continue as long as those who have chosen them believe that the doctor, lawyer, executive, or mayor is serving their best interest and has their welfare in mind at all times. In other words, the arrangement is contingent upon a basis of trust.

The idea of being employed by a church is hardly acceptable to a Pentecostal minister because of the inference of being a hireling. But we use this terminology only to describe the working relationship between church and pastor, not with regard to spiritual authority. When the minister admits that he came to the church with their consent and is supported by them with the understanding that he advance their best spiritual interest, then this terminology may not be too far afield.

The minister is primarily a servant of the most high God. Not dictation from the pew, but revelation from above determines his pulpit utterances. He is to say, "What shall I do?" and "Speak; for thy servant heareth," to the Lord, not to the laity. (See I Samuel 3:10; Acts 22:10.) He is an ambassador of God, and the triumph of God's kingdom is his chief concern. Yet these considerations fail to alter the fact that a pastorate is a business relation, based on a contract between the preacher and the church that has secured his services. To meet every church engagement, to prepare for it carefully, to be prompt, to respond to every reasonable call, to be alert for opportunities, to allow no interference with his duties to the church, and to study so that he may serve the people better—these are matters of plain, ordinary business honesty. The church pays the pastor cold cash and in return has a right to expect diligent service.

Of course, the right kind of employee is seldom discharged. People will appreciate a minister who is trying to give them their money's worth.

As we have previously noted, people are the minister's stock and trade. They are the materials that he works with. His intent is to shape them into a product acceptable to the Lord. The success of a minister is determined by how he brings people to this ideal conformity.

It is said that a carpenter can be judged by his scrap pile. Perhaps we can apply somewhat the same evaluation to a preacher. The man of God who is able to shape vessels of honor from lives that may seem hopeless, has, to a large degree, mastered the fine art of pastoring. Experience teaches that some people cannot be fashioned into a workable, acceptable attitude and way of life. They resist the hand of the potter, even down to the firing in the oven. According to Jeremiah, such a vessel must be placed back upon the wheel or finally out into the potter's field. But here again, we must remember that the good potter has a small percentage of rejects and that in Jeremiah God is the potter who passes the final judgment. It is to the lasting credit of a pastor to be able to get along with people and, at the same time, lead them to conform to the divine image of the Lord.

James reminds us, "The fruit of righteousness is sown in peace" (James 3:18). Growing into the image of God will not take place except in the atmosphere of Christ-likeness. The foregoing verse of Scripture also stipulates the kind of person who sows the seeds of righteousness: "of them that make peace." The peacemaker invariably makes the best pastor.

There is a distinct place in society for the proper kind of revolutionist, but such a person is seldom able to fulfill the role of statesman also. After the revolution has run its course, and the uprooting and tearing down of old structures has been completed, its leaders are often unable to adapt themselves to reconstruction. It is one thing to destroy and another thing altogether to rebuild. It is the patient peacemaker who slowly harmonizes, constructs, and builds.

No one doubts that a church in turmoil cannot be a healthy, growing, productive church. For that reason, this chapter stresses some of the things that tend to produce harmony in a local assembly. This is not to imply that there are never times when adjustments must be made in a local assembly. And during the process of adjustment, there may be an upheaval, but it is God's will for the church to make the necessary changes and gain the desired results without a resulting explosion.

It is not good, of course, for a pastor to pursue the role of a pacifist always and forever, refusing to stand up in a problematic situation. There are times when the only honorable way to meet a situation is head-on. In this case, if the pastor has no personal feelings in the matter to affect his judgment, if he is in God's will, and if he has kept himself free from blame, most of the time the confrontation will turn out to the furtherance of God's kingdom. Since the worth of the preacher is judged by the churches he builds, rather than the ones he tears up, it is well to consider some of the things that makes for harmonious pastorates.

A Carnegie Institute survey showed that ninety percent of all people who failed in their job, did so because they were not able to get along with others at some stage of their working relationship. This could be true of ministers also. Some ministers have great pulpit ability and other abilities as well but seemingly cannot rise to the level of production of which they appear to be capable. A close examination of their lives might reveal that they lack the ability to get along with others. In the process of doing God's work, they stir up so much opposition against themselves that progress is impossible. More than one well-meaning preacher has consistently torn up as much or more than he was able to build. This, of course, finally produces nothing but failure, plus much misunderstanding and heartache. How sad to come to the end of life with nothing left standing to show for the years of hard toil!

Solving a problem that arises depends much on the minister's attitude toward the problem and the person involved. If the person involved feels, justifiably or not, that the minister is against him personally, the likelihood of reaching a solution is almost nil. At once, he is thrown on the defensive and in a position of distrust.

However, if the minister can thoroughly wash his mind and heart in love, looking upon the parishioner with compassion as someone who needs help and divorcing himself from any personal prejudice in the matter, he enhances the likelihood that he can accomplish some good. If the layperson who counsels with the pastor feels that he is speaking to a friend who is looking out for his welfare, he will have an open mind as to a possible solution instead of a closed door of guarded caution.

A minister of great ability had the besetting sin of invariably dividing all groups he had any association with. It was simply his method of leadership. He did not know how to bring harmony and weld opposing parties into a workable whole. As a result, what should have been a very fruitful ministry was marred by many battlefields, strewn with broken hearts and bitter memories. The most tragic thing was that many souls who could have been saved by the energy expended in the countless battles will no doubt come to the judgment still unsaved. Obviously, the peacemaker will, in the end, have more to show for his work than the well-meaning person who does not know the way of peace.

There can be no harmony unless the pastor is first at peace with himself. People who tend to become parties in problems have personal troubles of their own, relative to their personality and attitude, that have remained unsolved over the years. These problems take the form of inferiority complexes, inhibitions, and various shades of fear and insecurity. Most of them are products of home environment or early training. They add up through the years and become part of the sum total of a person's emotional structure. People's reaction under a given circumstance is greatly determined by many prejudices, resentments, or unconscious associations that have built up in life. Often they do not make decisions by reason but by feelings. Unconscious guilt feelings surface, showing up as distaste or vehement denunciation. The person can be completely unaware that his reaction is the manifestation of a certain facet of his life of which he is ashamed. Of course, some things need to be denounced. But the person who understands himself is likely to be more humble in his judgments of right and wrong.

The preacher who is forever involved in some sort of squabble is not sure of himself or not at peace with himself. His many battles are often attempts to prove something to himself or to others. If he were filled with confidence, he would not feel the need to prove himself or his point. Here, we do not refer to obvious stands that ministers must take as a matter of course against compromise and wrong, but to personality clashes and misunderstandings among friends.

The person who causes this type of conflict usually harbors some sort of frustration, and he projects this frustration into his relationships. The person who is at peace with himself will project peace, while the person who is at war within himself will project disunity and turmoil.

Once, a very good man took a small village church where there were two inactive ministers, both of whom were also good people. Since they had been faithful to the congregation and of long residence in the local church, they had, over the years, acquired an honor and respect that created an awkward and unhealthy condition within the church family. Neither of the ministers was aware that the allegiance they received from the people began to put the new pastor in an uncomfortable position. The pastor, because of his own personality, needed the assurance and trust that the other ministers enjoyed. Local conditions aggravated a sense of insecurity and suspicion, ultimately resulting in an explosion that brought hurt to several people. Perhaps there could have been another way of adjusting the situation if

219

the pastor had possessed the necessary confidence in his ability.

Blessed is the preacher who can take a calm, rational view of any given problem, not only considering all its pros and cons but also judging his own feeling toward the matter, asking unsparingly, "Why do I feel toward this situation as I do?" If a situation is wrong, the preacher should judge it to be so, but he should give his judgment in such a way that it does not create adverse reactions in the parties who receive it. While the moral rectitude of principles is so important, those principles must be presented and received in the right spirit if they are to lead to salvation. If a pastor applies them in a way that does not make people better, he accomplishes very little good.

The approach of one well-known Pentecostal minister was very impressive. Some harsh incidents in his boyhood, such as having to pick up his breakfast from garbage cans while on his way to school, had left many harmful attitudes and complexes. But through the years he had tried to understand why he reacted as he did under certain circumstances and even why he did certain things in bringing up his son. By coming to understand himself more fully, he was able to rise above attitudes and approaches that would have been very damaging to his ministry.

Fear is a dangerous force that often lurks inside the preacher. Fear can don the cloak of distrust, suspicion, envy, jealousy, and excessive worry. Until a person comes to the place where he can rest upon God and trust the future to Him, he is liable to be preyed upon by many corrosive emotions.

The minister needs to feel that while he may not have

as great a ministry as another brother, he has a ministry that is equally important in God's sight. He needs the assurance that God gave him his ministry and that as long as he lives and abides in the vine, there will be a place for him to exercise it. Nothing will ever come of his life except it be in the will of God, so he need do nothing other than his faithful best under all circumstances, and God will take care of the rest.

The minister who does not come to this attitude but allows fear to shadow him, will react to situations in ways that will later shame him. For instance, what one fears, he sometimes destroys. If a pastor directs his fear toward a member of his church, he will treat this person as a threat to his position, a potential enemy, and this attitude will affect his relationship with the individual. Clearly, then, the preacher must be at peace with himself, if he is to create a harmonious atmosphere in the church and a good working relationship with his church family.

Inward frustrations not only have their bearing on the pastor's relations to his church, but they also make a difference in his organizational standing and his ministerial fellowship. It has often been said that men are only grown-up boys. At least in some things this seems to be so. They never grow too old to need an outlet for self-expression. They consider that an acceptance of their expressions is an acceptance of themselves. Everyone has been embarrassed or amused by the attempts of children to gain recognition when company comes. The term "showing off" describes the various antics of children to secure attention. Grown-up boys make the same attempt but in a different way. This concept is not as ridiculous as it may sound, inasmuch as everyone is an egoist to some extent and wants acceptance by at least part of society.

Some methods that people choose for expression are constructive, helpful, and socially acceptable within the fellowship. By their very nature as well as conviction, however, other brethren may express themselves in a role of opposition relative to certain principles and practices. Opposition is not an evil thing in itself, inasmuch as everyone is entitled to his own opinions, and at times his opinions may be altogether right. Moreover, the fellowship needs expressions of disagreement for the sake of balance and exposure of both sides of a question. It is not unusual, though, in the process of debate and decision, for a good brother to unintentionally create for himself a negative image that may not portray his real character and personality. Quotes, prejudice, and hearsay can play a part in creating this image.

It is easy to say that one does not care what other people think, but this is just not true. Sooner or later, everyone cares a great deal what people think. It is worthwhile to ask if championing or opposing a certain issue is important enough to justify a commitment, before lending name and influence to a particular effort. Some things are not worth what they cost in influence and respect. Somebody will always be coming by with a flag, but the mature person does not march in everybody's band. He should decide the motives behind each issue. The principle itself may be right, but the whole concept can be dirtied and cheapened by backers whose motives are questionable.

When a righteous issue is represented wrongly, the solid preacher should neither disown the principle nor remain neutral on the matter. He is wise to keep quiet in circles where his name may be used unfairly. If he cannot present his views honestly, with a good spirit, and to a righteous advantage, it is better to leave them unsaid. If the temperature is already high on a given question, it needs nothing that he can add unless it is reasoning. If he is in company of those who do not appreciate a reasonable approach, it is better for him to keep his opinions to himself. He should speak privately with those who may be of a contrary opinion. He should also speak before the committees or other bodies that may be responsible for forming policy relative to the point in question.

The wise, peace-loving minister desires always to remain his own, not allowing his name to become the property of an agitated group who wishes to promote something by questionable means. A mature minister who has the same convictions as an opposition group, will place his words and influence where they will count most, in the proper place and at the proper time. No one worth his salt could remain altogether quiet when principles of right and wrong are in the balance. But neither will he allow his name and quotes to be used unfairly. It takes too long to build a ministry, a reputation, and a righteous image to hand them out simply for the asking.

A man of peace knows that contending for righteous principles in an unrighteous way will not produce righteous results. The solid, well-balanced Pentecostal preacher will preach and strongly uphold all the standards of our fellowship but also realize that "the fruit of righteousness is sown in peace of them that make peace." He should usually be able to live in peace with the brethren of the same organizational fellowship.

The executive in any phase of responsibility knows

the value of attempting to understand the people who oppose him. This is absolutely necessary if he is to ever reach an agreement with them. Once he recognizes what makes his opposition tick, when he discovers not only what irritates them but why it does so, then he has gained insight into the heart of the problem. Not only does knowing the background of the problem assist in arriving at a solution, but it gives the pastor the patience to plod toward the solution. The third blessing of understanding is to help the person who is in opposition. When he comes to feel that he is understood, at least half of the battle is won.

Understanding one's opposition does not come about unless a person has a great desire to understand. The problem itself becomes strictly secondary, and the man or woman involved becomes all important. When the person who is in opposition or who is being counseled is convinced that the pastor has his welfare at heart, many of the mental and emotional blocks that would otherwise make an understanding impossible are immediately taken away. After all, the desire of most people is to be understood.

Trust is a valuable ingredient in a harmonious relationship between the pastor and his church. Scripture asks the question, "Can two walk together, except they be agreed?" (Amos 3:3). A partnership will not continue long if the two partners find it impossible to trust one another. A high percentage of marriages that end in divorce arrive at such a state because either the husband or wife does not trust the other. The failure of many pastorates originates in an event that precipitated distrust between the pastor and the congregation.

Sometimes congregations do not trust their minister because of an unpleasant experience they had with a another preacher, perhaps dating back for many years. Once, a congregation was sold under the table to an incoming pastor at so much per head. For years they deeply resented being treated as so much chattel to be sold at will. It is no wonder that they compiled a church government of their own that stymied the growth of the church and made it impossible for any self-respecting man of God to continue long as their pastor.

Strong church boards are often the result of a broken trust between the church and a preacher in times past. The tragedy is that sometimes years must past for this fear to be allayed and for the church to realize that bylaws concerning the pastor-church relationship will never take the place of simple trust in the pastor who endeavors to lead them.

Trust is so easily broken but so very hard to build back again. Those who are responsible for shattering Christian confidence between pastor and church will have to wait until eternity to know the full extent of the damage they have done. How foolish any preacher is who thinks that he can maintain a church by sleight of hand and undercover maneuverings! Many pastors have decided that it was far better to endure inconvenience in some things for a time, and later gain their objectives straight across the table as a willing gesture of trust, than to obtain their desires sooner at the cost of the congregation's faith in their integrity. After all, everyone expects a preacher to be a gentleman and a Christian. Without a doubt, when a congregation discovers that their pastor is less than that, their trust in him is broken.

In a previous chapter, we set forth the scriptural truth of spiritual authority. Ideally, as New Testament practices show, the ministry is to rule the church and lead them in the will of God. However, there is a difference between an ideal and its application to a local situation. Matching the ideal of authority with the exercise of authority under local circumstances is not as simple as it may seem.

The term *authority* has an appeal to a leader and especially to one who does not understand that *responsibility* always travels in the same company. Authority does not always guarantee a clearly understood and respected position, as some have thought. There are many instances in which authority is not effective. In fact, the violation of authority is often accepted as a matter of course, and its implications are not considered.

We are often appalled at the extent of major criminal activities. Strengthening the enforcement agencies of government does not always rectify these violations of law, for raw strength itself does not always ensure obedience to authority. In totalitarian states, where personal liberty is at a minimum and arbitrary authority is at a maximum, many people still violate laws on a wide scale. In short, real authority does not depend solely upon the amount of force that an organization can bring to bear.

What Pentecostal church does not have people in it who repeatedly violate certain standards of the church, even while they profess to recognize formal authority? All members of United Pentecostal Churches are supposed to maintain family devotions, but who is so naive as to say that all Pentecostal families do so? So we see the difference between the ideal and actual exercise of and submission to authority.

Much of the time, people will obey or disobey specific rules according to whether they receive an advantage or a disadvantage by obeying them. Personal consecration, love for God, and respect for church and leadership are all factors in their judgment as to whether to obey a particular teaching or decision. Any mature pastor will acknowledge that no authority can compel the quality of membership participation that will produce a spiritual good. There can be no practical authority without a corresponding feeling of responsibility on the part of those who receive the directives. A saint must feel a moral responsibility in order for him to truly follow authority.

Consciously or unconsciously, saints understand that authority does not rest ultimately in the pastor who makes certain requests of them, but in God who called him into the ministry. If they believe that the pastor is scripturally right and in the will of God, and if they reverence his position, then his authority becomes a personal force in their lives, hard to resist. So whether they comply with a certain rule or not does not depend merely on its issuance, but on the choice that they make in their hearts. And as we have already stated, the attitude of a person toward God, His Word, and the ministry will color his decision. The ultimate power of the directive lies with the people who receive the directive, and not in the ruling that is issued. The decision as to whether an order has authority or not lies with the persons to whom it is addressed, not with the one who issues the order.

As a practical matter, then, a pastor's assurance that his congregation will follow him is based on the amount of trust in their hearts for him and his God. Whether authority is of personal or institutional origin, it is created and maintained by public opinion, which in turn is conditioned by sentiment, affection, reverence, awe, and sometimes, for a while, fear. When these conditions no longer exist, the preacher's authority is gone. He retains his ideal authority under God in the ministry, but the proper environment for practical authority no longer exists, and therefore it cannot function.

For this reason, it is of great practical value for a pastor to live in trusting harmony with his congregation. This is not to suggest that in order to have peace a pastor must be a hireling or must continually pacify his church. Who could respect such a leader? It is possible to have both strong, capable leadership and peace at the same time. In fact, they complement one another. Church trouble does not complement a minister, yet there may be times when the man of God cannot avoid making adjustments within the structure of his church. The peaceable pastor, however, is grieved by unavoidable unrest and cannot bring himself to glory in a strong position he had to take.

For a minister to boast of trouble in his church is as reasonable as a father boasting about the critical illness of his child. Even an amputation, though a choice between life and death, is not something that a person would actually desire if another option were possible. Certainly no right-thinking father would boast about his child's being an amputee. The right-thinking minister looks upon disfellowshiping a saint as the last resort and in some measure an admission of his own lack of success in not being able to reconcile and rectify estranged lives.

One of the greatest producers of harmony in a church is progress. Genuine progress is one thing that is impossible to argue with. The shouts of newborn babes in

Christ and the splashing of water in the baptismal tank go a long way toward quieting the voice of the dissenter.

A congregation may be unusually placid or patient and adjust itself to a lack of progress, but the average group of people responds with joy and rallies behind the pastor who is leading the church to victory. Old ills are more easily forgotten and long-existing church cliques are soon outnumbered when strong, positive growth takes place. In time, it no longer becomes necessary to lean so heavily upon people whose judgment and feeling toward certain things may be warped or prejudiced. New people with fresh faith and vision come to the front, bringing strength and vibrancy to the entire church.

Knowing this, it is not unusual for a new pastor to seek to inaugurate his pastorate with notable achievements. Several factors give rise to this urge. First impressions are important. All eyes are fixed on him. The board who recommended him to the church eagerly awaits a justification of their judgment. The people are expectant, believing him to be a gifted man of God. So, feeling that he should "make hay while the sun shines," the new pastor plunges into his work. This is just as it should be. However, there are a few things that it is well for him to bear in mind at this point.

The pastor can commit serious mistakes in the first year—or any other year—by letting zeal get ahead of wisdom. Many have observed that if a pastor rushes things too much in the first year, then the ordinary sequel is a desire or demand for a resignation in the third year. Many seeds of unhappy pastorates are planted in the first six months by undue haste for results. Many times a new pastor, unaware of obstacles, launches enterprises that collapse. Not seeing the pitfalls, he suddenly finds himself in most unfortunate positions. Failing to discern the important needs, he wastes his time on the inconsequential.

Two situations justify an immediate crash program of change by the new pastor. First, the church may be in such a depressed or crippled condition that only emergency measures can prevent immediate dissolution. Circumstances may arbitrarily limit the pastorate to a year or less, thus calling for early activity. Second, there are times when the ripeness of an opportunity, and the popular demand of the congregation for immediate action, may justify the quick launching of a new enterprise, but two dangers are at hand.

First, if the new pastor makes major changes immediately, he sets a high-water mark of achievement at the very outset of his pastorate that may be hard to live up to later. Second, if he is not well acquainted with the people whom he will be working closely with, he may make some mistakes relative to those he uses or does not use.

A pastorate that begins with a rush and then tapers off in declining interest is marked in public opinion as a half failure. Of course, we must evaluate all these things in the light of God's leading. In a Pentecostal church, the minister should be ready for revival at any time. What preacher is not ready for a harvest of souls at any time that the Spirit seems to move in that direction? But our comments about rapid change refer primarily to the more natural side of the church, such as building programs, promotions, and major revamping of the church structure.

A certain law of the harvest prevails in the church. If progress is to be continual, year after year, there must also be a commensurate sowing, tilling, fertilizing and

watering year after year. When a minister tells of a great harvest of souls during the first year of his pastorate, we can often rightly conclude that another has labored faithfully before him, and he has entered into that labor. The credit, then, is not primarily his, but it belongs to the one who was there before him. Of course, he should immediately reap such a harvest, no matter how young the pastorate, but what about future years? That depends on his tilling of the soil, since every year the soil must be prepared for future crops. How many cases can we recall where preachers had large additions to their churches the first year, fewer the second, and none the third? And the fourth? There usually is no fourth! Such pastorates are short-lived. Where the plow and harrow are not employed, the reaper will not be needed long.

What farming implements should the pastor employ? Effective tools are healthy Sunday school work with trained teachers; well-organized follow-up and visitation programs; sincere, warmhearted preaching that appeals directly to the needs of the congregation; and down-to-earth friendliness on the part of the pastor and his wife toward everyone in general and those with spiritual needs in particular.

It has been aptly stated, "All the world loves a lover." The genuine love that a preacher has in his heart for everyone will not fail to manifest itself in many and varied ways even within the first year of his pastorate. He will not lightly pass over the small things that show his interest in the unsaved families who are connected in some way with the church. In this way, the wise pastor will not only demonstrate his personal love for people but will also spread goodwill both for himself and for the

Christ he represents.

Of course, attempting to show an interest where no occasion for it exists is futile and may seem foolish, but when something unusual occurs in their lives, people crave manifestation of interest from their friends. A telephone call helps a little. A letter, written sincerely, is better, but usually a personal call means more. This kind of call is a response to a special situation that offers the opportunity of manifesting personal interest in the life of a person who may not be as close to the church and God as he should be, or to a sinner the minister is trying to win. Of course, sickness, sorrow, misfortune, or death create a desire for sympathy. Similarly, success, honor, and the anticipation of special pleasure, such as a vacation, offer the opportunity for a congratulatory call. It is perhaps strange, but true, that people want to share their joys as well as their sorrows.

A minister's wife once questioned the need for a visit her husband was about to make, saying that the family he was calling on did not expect it from him. "That's exactly why I am going," was his reply. His theory was that the unexpected and unusual service of a minister would never be forgotten. He was right. The call a minister makes to admire a new car, to look over a new home, to pray with a young person in the home just before he goes away to college or military service; the short call the night before a family leaves for vacation, to pray for their safety—all these go a long way in creating goodwill and winning the lost. These efforts on the part of the pastor, consistently practiced, are a continual sowing of seed, and they will result in periodic harvest if he waters them well with prayer, the Word, and the walk of the Spirit.

If a pastor is to know the full measure of progress that brings harmony, he must be enthusiastic. This does not necessarily mean that he is to be a pronounced extrovert, but inside of him must be the sure, sound conviction that what he is doing is right and that it will succeed. Enthusiasm is contagious. If the preacher has it and can keep it in spite of setbacks and discouragement, his program is almost certain to succeed. Other leaders may have enthusiasm for a particular product or principle, but no leader can experience enthusiasm as a preacher can. All other claims of superiority fade into insignificance beside the eternal verities of the gospel and what it offers humanity. There is no limit to the heights of enthusiasm to which a preacher can allow his spirit to soar relative to the great work of God.

The convictions of a preacher must be strong if he is to convince others of their worth and to change their lives. The strength of his leadership is closely related to the conviction he has of the worthiness of his word and work. In addition to the Bible itself, the preacher's best arguments for action are the experiences of his own life. He knows what works and does not work, for he has proved them for himself. His personal experiences illustrate the truths of God's Word. In addition, he has observed other people's lives and has witnessed that the truth of the Bible applied to human lives is truth indeed. He knows full well, without the shadow of a doubt, that some things do not work. Thus on many subjects the preacher can speak with tremendous conviction. Other leaders, however capable, do not have access to the driving force and power that prompts the preacher. His conviction is part of the explosive enthusiasm needed to spark progress in a local church. Enthusiasm is an important ingredient in the mixing bowl of harmony.

In seeking progress, a pastor should realize that a good program can fail to get off the ground or receive congregational acceptance simply because he does not present it in the proper manner. It is harmful for a pastor to fall on his face in trying to promote a project that he believes is worthy of the congregation's acceptance. There is no substitute for a positive approach in presenting anything. Most of the time the full details of a project are a long time evolving in the mind of the busy pastor. He gives them his full thought from time to time, and, in the meantime, they remain in the back of his mind. Without his being conscious of it, he evaluates the various possibilities and weighs the opposing merits and demerits of each facet. It has been aptly said that anything that cannot be prayed about should not be done. One of the first things a preacher should do with a proposed undertaking in his church is to pray about it. He should soak it well in prayer, asking God to lead him, to put the right things into his mind and heart, and, if this proposal would prove harmful, to take the desire for it out of his mind.

He should ask God to analyze his heart and tell him if his motive for initiating the change is in any way tinged with selfishness or pride. In time, if he feels no check of the Spirit, but rather a quiet assurance from God that this step is in His will and time, he then should methodically begin to explore all the possibilities in its favor. He should do so as exhaustively as he can, and each time he thinks of another point, he should write it down. Then he should also write down all the reasons why this project should not be pursued, and then attempt to refute them. The minister should not be prejudiced. If the evidence indicates that the proposal might at that time be unwise, of course he should drop it. This is not hard to do if the minister has followed the suggested course and has not verbally committed himself to a course of action before he has explored all the possibilities.

If, after this period of prayerful evaluation, the pastor feels that he should enact the project at that time, he should begin at once to organize his thoughts, writing them out in detail and then outlining them, placing his strongest arguments at the last. When the time comes for him to stand before either the board or his congregation, he should come without apology but with a happy, optimistic view. He then unfolds his plan in an orderly, understandable way. He speaks slowly and emphatically so that all can understand. He knows what conclusion he wishes from his congregation, and, since he has done his homework well, he is sure of getting it. He will not worry about a lack of enthusiasm in his congregation at the start of his presentation, for he knows that it will build as time goes on; and it does, for he is well prepared, strong in his convictions, and enthusiastic.

A good leader in action is a wonderful sight to behold. He fulfills a dual role: pointing out the way of progress and, at the same time, resolving discord.

There can be no harmony, nor can there be actual spiritual progress, unless the people of a congregation develop the habit of prayer. Pentecost is not Pentecost without prayer. The Pentecostal preacher who does not pray cannot lead his people in prayer. Prayerless people are carnal people, and carnal people will use carnal methods in settling, or attempting to settle, the differences that invariably arise within a congregation. One pastor who strongly advocated prayer in his congregation explained simply, "If I can get my people to pray, I can get them to do anything." He was right. If for no other reason, the preacher should urge and lead his people to prayer in order to preserve harmony within his congregation. One Pentecostal pastor observed, "When my people begin to grow slack in their praying, I get afraid, because I know that anything can happen." Praying people are peaceable people!

Without doubt, it is the preacher's responsibility to lead his people in the practice of prayer. One good man who took a week to help a preacher friend of his with a church that was at a low spiritual ebb, advised his friend at the close of the week to begin a daily prayer meeting and continue it indefinitely. His friend agreed that the suggestion was good and added that he knew just whom to place in charge of the prayer meeting to ensure that it went on each day. The tart reply of the visiting brother was, "Forget it. If you are not going to be over it yourself, it is not worth starting, for it will not succeed anyway." Praying pastors in time beget praying churches.

Foresight and planning on the part of the pastor will encourage harmony and peace in a church congregation. If the church bulletin, bulletin board, or weekly announcements indicate that there is always something to look forward to, the congregation gets the idea that the pastor knows where he is going and that they are in the hands of someone who is giving to the church a sense of direction. But if weekend after weekend passes and nothing seems to be in the making other than routine services, uneasiness and frustration often take hold of the congregation, in a way that they themselves are at first unaware of. Bit by bit, the uneasiness grows until it surfaces in rumblings of discontent and questionings. A church does not have to be large to plan special efforts geared to the most conducive seasons of the year. Only the pastor can do this planning. Because of his position at the head, the church looks to him for this leadership and expects it of him. One layperson made this observation concerning his pastor, who had not been with the church very long: "Our former pastor was a better preacher, but this man is better for us because he has a program and carries it out."

For many pastors, the church year begins and ends in the fall. October marks the beginning of an attendance drive that they press intermittently by various means and ways through Easter. Then follows for others a loyalty campaign that includes the seven Sundays between Easter and Pentecost.

Pentecost Sunday lends itself greatly to an all-day observance, followed by a great evangelistic rally that night. It offers good material for publicity to direct the attention of the town to the claims and blessings of our message. Then there are youth camps, camp meetings, and other summer activities. Spaced through these months are anniversary services, revivals, and other special meeting. When these events are properly spaced, planned, and executed, they help carry the congregation through the year. By the design of God and the pastor, the activities of the church operate in such a way that, year by year, the people conform more and more to the image of Christ. As they keep busy in spiritual things, they develop harmonious relationships and share one with another. When a minister remains in a church year after year and witnesses continued growth and harmony, it is certain that much wise pastoring has gone into his work.

Wisdom to solve problems is a blessed thing, but more blessed is the rare wisdom of foreseeing problems and knowing how to avoid them. How true the old axiom, "An ounce of prevention is worth a pound of cure." Some mature pastors seem to have a sixth sense that enables them to smell out potential troubles before they have time to ferment, and thus they are able to move expertly to meet the need. Sore spots can develop in the church body and torment the whole, just as an infectious tooth incapacitates a person. It is so much better to prevent the decay or remove the cause than to put up with the pain forever. Pastoral care is much more desirable than removal.

Qualified leadership is the key to proper functioning of any program in the church. When the pastor starts a program, one of the first questions should be, Who will head this endeavor? If no one is qualified to head it, then the undertaking must wait until a suitable leader either moves into the congregation or is trained to assume that responsibility.

Another important question relative to a new program is, Will it conflict with existing programs? If it will, does its worth justify the supplanting of a previously existing program? Moreover, is the proposed program worthy of the time and effort that its promotion will demand? There is also personnel to consider. It may be that the people who ordinarily would be interested in or capable of working in such an endeavor are already overburdened with other church responsibilities. It is better to be realistic than to be embarrassed later. An inactive unit of church organization is awkward to explain and is embarrassing to the people responsible for it. It becomes a trouble breeder, a sore spot that the church would be better without.

Youth projects often begin with good intentions but soon die for the want of dedicated leadership and worthwhile objectives. The common cry, "Give the young people something to do," is radically wrong. It should be, "Give them something worthwhile to do." Projects that fail to present a challenge will, in time, be despised. Enjoyment itself is short-lived and does not produce lasting spiritual good, but rendering service to others blesses both the giver and the receiver. Youth activities that in some way involve spiritual service not only bless and strengthen the young people involved but have longer lives than those that end in self. When properly organized and supervised by someone who cares, services in rest homes, jails, and children's homes, as well as visits to shut-ins and to hospitals, are blessed and useful youth activities.

There comes a time in all churches when a certain function has ceased to be useful. At one time, perhaps, it had its place and contributed much to the church program, but the church may have outgrown it and developed a method of achieving the same result in a better way; or perhaps the people who originally felt the need of such a function are no longer part of the congregation. At any rate, inactive positions serve no good purpose and should either be reactivated or dispensed with.

The problem is how to go about adjusting certain situations without offending someone. Pruning looks easy and can be done quickly, but the results of hasty action may be around a long time to plague the pastor. The people who at one time benefited from a certain class, department, or function, hate to see it merged or replaced with some other approach to the same objective. They wonder why others should be robbed of the blessings they enjoyed. They think, Why not revive instead of destroy? Then the officers and members of that class or department certainly have to be considered. The officers may feel that its eradication is a reflection on their leadership, which will now be stamped as a failure. Even if they approve, there is a danger of their losing interest in other parts of the church work and cynically asking about other departments, "How long will they let this live?"

Before the pastor hastily reorganizes or eliminates a department, especially if his action will involve the juggling of personnel, it would be well for him to take care of a few things first. He should be careful about his timing. If he initiates action when the backwash will affects another important function of the church, such as a revival or a Sunday school drive, then he causes harm, and the change is all the more obvious. It is better for the pastor to announce far ahead of time that certain changes are being considered, with the hope of working out better arrangements. After a while, he can say that plans are being formed relative to certain procedures, and step by step, over a period of time, he can bring about the change without its coming as a shock.

If the pastor has heretofore manifested a real interest in the ailing department and has tried to lend his support in times past, little can be said about his not caring later when the change is made. If he has listened with sympathy to the problems of those involved before the action was taken, he will be seen as a friend rather than a foe. It may be that during such talks, he can ask for practical suggestions from those who feel the embarrassment of the lagging department. If changes come as their idea, then any potential for trouble is greatly allayed. Indeed, this process can arouse enthusiasm for a rearrangement that enables people to do the same work or accomplish the same goal more simply and effectively.

This process of change takes time—a few weeks if it involves a committee, a few months if it involves a department, a year or two if it involves a major change in the organizational structure of the church. One good pastor wanted to rearrange the baptistery in a certain way but met opposition. He could have insisted on his way at the outset of the proposal, but he delayed decision and let the whole thing rest. After a time, the very ones who opposed his initial proposal recommended that it be done.

Blessed is the preacher who discovers that he has every advantage in putting across his programs. He is the one who is continually before the people. Those who oppose him are at a great disadvantage. He has more time to contact and visit members than anyone else in the congregation. Then, too, time is on his side. The congregation changes over time; if he is able to keep peace and cultivate love and understanding, it will change in his favor.

The wise pastor soon finds that there is little need to throw an entire church into upheaval in order to have his way. He knows that sooner or later he can have his way without the trouble. It is better to spend two years preparing for an amputation than two years in healing the running sore caused by premature surgery. If a pastor will be wise enough to bide his time, he will be able to have harmony and eventually his own way also.

By far, the most dangerous change a pastor can make is the removal of an inefficient and unworthy official. Every church at some time has had certain officers in its various organizations who were qualified, some who were mediocre, and a few who were altogether out of place. Where rotation in office is the rule, wisdom allows that procedure to accomplish the change. The suggested local church government in the manual of the United Pentecostal Church International allows for a wonderful arrangement, since the pastor is the one who makes certain appointments, subject to ratification by the church. Under this setup, the pastor can rotate various officials of the church at the yearly business meeting. Many good pastors have used this convenient method to change ineffective officers as well as to give other capable and willing people a chance to share in the official responsibility of the church.

Once a church gets used to this rotation arrangement, they feel that it is only fair to practice it, because it prevents the management of the church from remaining in the hands of perhaps one or two predominant families and leaves it in the hands of all. Of course, there are some positions, such as the teaching staff, that should not and could not be replaced each year. The simple knowledge that all offices of the church are vacant once each year, with the exception of the pastor and perhaps the trustees, and that all officers are subject to reappointment or replacement, can take the sting out of change in this area.

Pastors who rotate one or more church board members every year, have found that the people are usually more satisfied with this arrangement and that the pastor can exercise firmer leadership of the church. When the church board has some changes each year, some pastors feel more free to rely on the board, inasmuch as the yearly changes will lessen the likelihood of their becoming power conscious and usurping pastoral authority.

Where a church does not automatically rotate board members, any change in board members requires much care. Personalities are perilous, and there are several danger points: (1) the official himself, (2) his family, (3) his friends, (4) the people opposed to his leadership, and (5) the general public. Somebody is bound to be hurt; some loss may be incurred. Unless the loss can be minimized, it may overbalance the gain of the change, and the final state will be worse than before.

In replacing someone who has been in office for a long time, the pastor should do his best to secure a superior successor, both in ability and in spiritual qualities, if at all possible. If the position goes to an inferior leader, there will certainly be trouble. Even an equal could be inadequate if the criticism becomes very pronounced. Certainly the pastor should try to avoid filling the vacancy unilaterally. Sometimes an ejected official has become a merciless critic and lifelong enemy. If, however, the office goes to an able, popular, or at least highly respected member whose consecration and sincerity are unquestioned and whose fitness justifies the choice, then critical mutterings will soon die down.

On these points, the pastor should not take public opinion lightly. People naturally sympathize with a person who has served long and faithfully and who is suddenly put out of his position. Once, a distressed member of a church, who was very much in sympathy with his pastor, called. It so happened that a board member who for years had not been faithful in church attendance had conspired to bring the pastor under the heavy hammer of judgment and criticism. Public opinion was on the side of the board member, so far as his position was concerned, since he had been in office for so long, so there was nothing that the good man of God could do but take it. However, he happened to be a mature Christian who could love in spite of rebuff, and he knew, as a leader, that losing a few battles did not necessarily mean losing the war. He went ahead with his pastoring, and in a few more years his leadership was stronger than ever before.

If a church has not had the practice of rotating board members but the pastor wants to institute it, he should take care how he does so. If it appears that he is only using it as a tool to get even with someone that he has a personal grudge against, it will backfire upon him. Personal grudges cannot be justified by the Word of God. Unless the congregation is convinced that adequate cause exists for the ousting of a longtime official, this action will arouse resentment against the initiators and, at times, even against the church itself.

Time is on the side of the well-meaning, wise pastor. Often when a suggestion is first made to replace a certain official in the church, it is best to postpone the action at once. After a year goes by, others will perhaps see the problem, especially if, in the meantime, they have received teaching about the ideal operation of the position. Even the friends of the individual may grow restless with him, especially if no one has made his office an issue and there is no reason to believe that the pastor is out to get him. It is much better if the pastor can wait and let public opinion be brought to bear before he makes the change. When the congregation fully realizes that there needs to be a change, and when the change is made with all gentleness and Christian grace, the pastor can accomplish it successfully.

Through sheer determination, a pastor could make many changes in the church, but it is best for him to make only the necessary changes without generating opposition against himself. After all, people are his business, and he should focus his actions on remaking lives and leading them toward God.

Certainly the pastor should avoid questionable political methods. He should also give the fullest recognition to the service and sacrifice of an officer who is being replaced. He should give something more than a perfunctory vote of thanks to retiring officers. If honor is due, it should be bestowed in full measure. While sincerity is important, equally important is generosity to brothers in Christ who may be hurt by their removal. Bungling with the surgeon's knife is dangerous business, especially when it is in the King's business.

Perhaps fewer officials of the church would need to be removed if pastors would take more time personally with them in communication and training. Many times people who are incapable of filling a particular office would be glad to qualify themselves if they had the opportunity. Jesus gave much time to His secondary leaders. He divided His time between the lost and suffering of the cities and the men who were to shoulder the responsibility of His church. In the Gospels, Jesus spoke often to His apostles about their tasks and braced them for the future by telling them what they could expect by way of opposition. He was their friend and their partner right down to the end, giving them the promise that He would be with them, never to forsake them. Jesus knew the value of a close working relationship between Himself and those He led.

If a pastor wants to get the best out of the leaders under him, he should cultivate a basic friendship that is warm and personal. There is a tremendous art to successful, capable leadership. Anyone who sees the artful procedures of good leadership will have keen admiration for those who have the maturity and the gentleness to exercise it.

The good leader knows that he should never do anything that he has already delegated to someone else, even though he may be able to do it far better. Instead, he must train the person who has the responsibility for the task, so that he can discharge adequately what he has been asked to do. If this individual cannot ever come up to full expectations, the pastor should quietly and carefully begin to seek his replacement. In doing so, he is being much more a friend than if he simply bypassed that office, for that action embarrasses an officeholder and takes away his dignity. Once the pastor has bypassed an office and performed the task himself, he has killed the effectiveness of that office and added another pound or two to the load he already carries. Furthermore, offices that do not function tend to become cancers in the church body. No office can remain healthy, aggressive, and effective unless it is duly recognized and used in the purpose for which it was created.

There is a distinct value in the pastor's keeping the confidence of his leaders. They should feel that he, above all others, is someone they can go to in time of distress and when their problems are more than they can handle. If they are to be confident in discharging their responsibilities, they must feel that their pastor will back them up personally if need be.

There is not a preacher living today who, though he has preached strongly and conscientiously, and in spite of all his good intentions, has not made some enemies who will go to their grave disliking him. This situation is a thorn in the side of peaceable preachers, something they never get used to. A minister's work is best accomplished by making friends, and undoubtedly he has more friends than any other employment would have brought him. These friends help offset the few enemies he has made through the years.

It is not unusual for some parishioners not to like the minister's preaching or personality, and others will dislike him for other reasons, but this situation need not trouble him, provided that these people constitute a small minority. He does not relish it, but he can put up with it. If, however, he has some real enemies who are bitterly hostile and determined to secure his overthrow, let him beware. Two or three influential men in his church can thwart his efforts and make his pastorate so uncomfortable that, in time, he will either engage in an open power struggle or move out from under the pressure.

Personal confrontation with malicious people is dangerous, and a preacher should approach it with extreme care and prayer, remembering that "we wrestle not against flesh and blood" (Ephesians 6:12). When his enemies are wrapped in flesh and are called by men's names, there is danger of his straying outside God's permissive will.

Seldom does a preacher win in a head-on personal struggle. Time, strategy, God, and the Word of God will accomplish a cleaner, more satisfactory settlement than a knockdown, drag-out conflict. This is not to say that drastic measures are never in order, but their application is seldom needed. There are some situations in which a church cannot survive without drastic surgery. Under such circumstances, blessed is the leader who has the courage, reluctantly and with fear, to wield the knife, and woe to the one who has a malicious love for bloodletting.

Ministers are only being honest when they admit that some of their enemies are primarily of their own making and that they could have avoided some conflicts. If a minister is not prayerful and spiritual, he can at times develop a dislike toward some people. Their manners, spirit, words, and actions become unpleasant to him, perhaps even offensive. That dislike may grow into indignation and scorn. It may develop into real enmity and in a few cases give rise to hatred. The cause may be their treatment of him, his family, his friends, or his church. When they discover his feelings, as they will, they will reciprocate.

If a minister dislikes someone, despises him, or hates him, in some cases that person will feel the same toward the minister. What if he has no grounds for such feelings? That makes no difference. Like begets like. When a minister speaks bitterly against men and women in his congregation, one may safely assume that sooner or later they will return the "compliment" with compound interest. It is a great mistake to sow to the wind, for one who does so will reap the whirlwind.

Unfortunately, such a reaction can occur even when a

parishioner only imagines that the minister dislikes him. A minister should exercise extreme care toward someone who has treated him shamefully. He must, by all means, show, as soon as possible, that he did not take affront to this treatment and that he is still his friend. (See Matthew 5.) The person who has mistreated a minister goes on the defensive, for he assumes that the man of God despises him. Sometimes he will seek to regain his self-respect by believing and proclaiming that the preacher did even worse things. It is wise not to justify his accusation by retaliatory actions.

There is only one remedy in this case: we are to love people as Jesus Christ has commanded. We should accept them for the poor soil they are and continue to sow the seed, blind to their unattractive qualities, forgetting their foolish and unkind words, forgiving their mean actions. We must rise higher and put into practice all that the Master commanded concerning attitudes and actions toward enemies.

A minister who finally makes up his mind to go into an open, bitter power struggle with an individual or faction in his church had better be ready to pay the price. His ministry, family, income, and reputation are at stake. As we have already stated, there may be a few instances in which such an action is necessary, but the experience is certainly not one to be coveted.

There is always the danger that the church will not stand behind their minister. How often a young man has said, "Oh, but the people are all with me," only later to find himself deserted and defeated! There are several reasons for this. The majority of people do not like to be in a fight, especially a church fight, and when the battle comes, they remain at home. They have their homes in that town and plan to live there the rest of their lives. They do not like the idea of regularly having to face on the streets the person they have taken a stand against, while the preacher may have long since taken his departure.

Most of them, moreover, realize from the first, as the minister might not, that it is a lost cause. They are closer to the situation in some measure than the preacher, having people say things to them that they would not say to the preacher. They may know that there is not even a fighting chance. Nobody wishes to enlist for a retreat. The main reason, however, is that they consider it his fight, not theirs.

Tragic, indeed, is the minister who has more enemies than he has friends. It is true that Jesus made enemies, and they drove Him from Nazareth, imprisoned Him, and finally crucified Him. But all of this was in the course of evangelism. Modern stonings and crucifixions, strangely do not often occur in the marketplaces, administered by the hands of this world, but by those who are supposed to be working with the church.

Not all of these circumstances are the fault of the preacher, but it is advantageous for him to be honest and to accept the blame of the enemies that he does unwisely create. He can wait for time to bring to pass a certain project that he desires, but hatred against him takes a long time and much effort to eradicate. A politician, even a statesman, can have many enemies and still move on from victory to victory; but a minister in a church cannot carry on if he has many enemies among the leaders of his church. It is impossible, in such an atmosphere, for the pastor to take care of the job he was called to do.

Let us remember: "The fruit of righteousness is sown in peace of them that make peace" (James 3:18). Peaceful harmony in a church is a precious jewel indeed.